Darkness in Summer

Translated by Cecilia Segawa Seigle

Darkness in Summer

Takeshi Kaiko

Charles E. Tuttle Company
Tokyo

Darkness in Summer

I know thy works, that thou art neither cold nor hot:
I would thou wert cold or hot.

BOOK OF REVELATION
CHAPTER 3, VERSE 15

In those days I was still doing some traveling.

I had just left one country and entered another. Sleeping and waking, I passed one day after the next in a cheap hotel in the students' quarter of the capital city. It was the beginning of summer, most of the inhabitants had already gone south on vacation, and the city was deserted, like a vast cemetery or an empty valley. Every day, the rain began in the morning and the sky hung low like an old, greasy wad of cotton. There was no warmth or brilliance anywhere. Summer was ailing with some terrible incontinent sickness and there was nothing but the cold, wet, and dark. There was no sense of burgeoning life or growth. That appealed to me.

A river flowed in front of the hotel, and a cathedral stood on the opposite bank amid a grove of trees. Whenever I looked, the river was a muddy gray-yellow and dimpled by numerous raindrops, and the gargoyles of the cathedral roof were drenched. The gargoyles had frozen in the midst of turning around to roar; having been stared at, they had turned into stone. I sat on the bed, sipping vodka, and watched the circles continuously expanding and then disappearing across the surface of the yellow river. And as I stared, the fungus threads of the rain soon vanished, and it seemed as though only one solid stream of rain was falling. I would become bored with it after a while and fall asleep. Waking, I would go out to buy bread and ham, not even stopping at bookshops, movie theaters, or restaurants. I would return to eat in bed, and then sleep some more. It seemed as though my body had disappeared and my brain had melted away; I could go on sleeping endlessly no matter how much I had already slept.

The room was in a students' boardinghouse. The old wallpaper had been torn here and there, and was streaked with brown bloodstains, apparently traces of crushed bedbugs. The mirror in the bathroom had a large Y-shaped crack; there was a bathtub, in which hot water was only occasionally available. A bed and a table crowded the room, so that one had to turn sideways to pass between them. Red curtains resembling burlap bags hung over the window. They imparted a blood-red cast to the entire room, whenever I switched on the small, old, tulip-shaped lamp, and the desert faded out, leaving only a soft warm gentleness. Shadows of cliffs, forests, caves, and skies took form on the walls and ceiling. While watching, smoking a bitter cigarette made of pickled black leaves wrapped in corn paper, I would begin to doze again, although I had only just awakened. No one knocked; no telephone rang; no books, no discussion. I continued to sleep in my red cocoon. My cheeks and stomach bulged with pale, flabby fat, and whenever I woke I felt as though I were wearing a mask. Imprisoned in heavy flesh, I would try to digest the memories of the past ten years, but I would only be overcome by lassitude, and all difficulties and joys would lose their substance, appearing like dusky shadows and distant landscapes. The lassitude proliferated like a greenhouse vine that has run over from a flowerpot onto the floor, and still continues to grow even though it has not the strength to lift stem or leaf. The vitality that evaporated from my body crawled over the walls, sprawled across

(4

the ceiling, filled the room, and thrived like an internal confusion. Strands of monologues, words, and concepts entangled themselves without any connection; they entwined, opened leaves, and reached out with grasping tentacles.

When going out to buy bread, if the rain happened to diminish, I would climb the gentle slope of the boulevard leading to the park. I took secret pleasure in watching one not-quite old man working there. I would sit on a bench a little away from him. Whenever I was in the city, I had to check whether he was still in good health. I had done so the previous year and also three years before. He must have earned a fair living doing this same work over the past several years; compared to the first time I had seen him, his abdomen had grown round and protruding, and bags had formed under his eyes. His back was stooped. But his art, which consists of swallowing and spitting out a frog, which he keeps in a fishbowl, is now much more refined. As preparation, he drinks water in the shade of a tree; when he sees pedestrians approaching, he appears on the road, opens his mouth wide, and suddenly dangles his large, thick tongue covered with yellow-green fur. He places a frog on it and gulps it down. He blinks his eyes, raises his right hand, and hits his potbelly fiercely with the edge of his hand. Water gushes out of his mouth, splashing all over, and dumping out the frog. Covered with gastric slime, the frog jumps around on the sand. The man picks it up again and returns it to the fishbowl. Then he stretches out his open palm to the audience. The spectators fumble in their pockets and place one or two coins in the man's hand and then leave absent-mindedly. Throughout the entire display, the man maintains his silence. He does not utter a sound, not even a snicker. He seems to earn a living by swallowing the frog and water and spitting them out so many times a day. He is not a deaf-mute, for I had spotted him drinking at a bar, fishbowl at his side, talking and laughing with the proprietor. I wonder if he didn't live through the war, swallowing and ejecting the frog for the masses of people who were rushing about in confusion. I wouldn't be surprised if it were his intention to do so until he died. Anyway, I have decided to believe he will. I feel content watching his total contempt. I cannot help giving a sigh of relief. I realize that there's a way out yet; and a way out such as this. I buy bread and ham at a store and return to my room, and, taking off the shirt and shoes I had just put on a few minutes ago, I fall back into my bed. The blanket has a mold, shaped by my body, and I fit right back into the shell. As soon as my cheek sinks into the pillow, drowsiness begins to rise like smoke. Bits and pieces, soft things, shapeless objects again begin to grow their leaves, stretch their vines, and fill the entire room.

Early one morning, I put on a windbreaker and went to the railroad station. It was empty and cold, and the night was still crawling in the twilight of the street corners, as though leaving begrudgingly. A large green shadow hung in the dark station and pink glints of light from the restaurant sparkled; but the walls were dismal and night and morning were surreptitiously vying with each other. The faces of men and women were either buried in wrinkles or evaporating at the edges of coffee cups. Many hitchhikers were crouched in sleep near the restaurant entrance, resting their heads on knapsacks or dufflebags; a tacky smell, like that of the dirt between toes, rose from their hair and necks, and they kept their watery eyes open blankly, dropping their chins on their chests and retiring completely into their pubic-hair-like mustaches, in ways that reminded one of soldiers who surrender before they see the enemy. I took a seat and asked for a hot rum. As the drops of hot rum, giving off a delicious aroma, soaked into the softened, tired folds of my intestines, each drop felt as though it were causing a flower to open. Underneath the stagnant fatigue, came the first slow stirring of anticipation. Then it started to grow rapidly, mingling with the rum and giving off vapors; it started to tower and began to hover over me without showing its face. She is coming by sleeping car; I wonder if she slept well . . .

. . . It's been ten years.

Roughly ten years. Everything is vague. I can't recapture it. My lethargy is beginning to take the upper hand again, though I am now in a crowd. Just the day before yesterday, when she sent me a telegram from the suburbs of the small capital of a neighboring country, my memories were reliable. I would pass the time in my blanket by constructing and reconstructing her voice, eyes, and surroundings, separating one scene and staring at it for hours. In the midst of flashing faces of numerous other women, one face loomed in the dusky light in front of them all. She laughed, arching her white throat, bit her thin lips, lowered her eyes, and brushed her hair from her forehead. But now all I can see is a small, distant scene of the day we parted, in the sweet aroma of the rum and the smoky fog of cigarettes. It was about eight in the evening, at a suburban station in Tokyo. Several times before, after meals and love-making, she had intimated a determination to leave Japan, but it was nothing more than a vague hint. She had not stated it as her clear intention, nor had she explained any details of her plans. I could only gather later, when her letters arrived from abroad, that she had been at a loss, not knowing what to tell me even if she had wanted to tell me anything at all. I did not say anything to her then, nor had I on any other occasion before that night. I just lay there, listening silently. I had never pried into matters that she had made no attempt to discuss, or simply did not wish to tell me. That had not changed even now. It was because other people's weakness made me feel insecure. I was unable to bear the weight of any responsibility. Sometimes hating and abhorring this overly strong attachment to myself, I was still incapable of lifting my face from it. I wonder if this lethargy bred ruthlessness. I struggled with her white, opulent breasts, drenched in perspiration, and her entire body was a furnace. In the meantime I was gazing into the short cypress hedge beyond the windows and listening to distant voices. I did not begin to grasp that she was bewildered by the limitless despair that quelled her boundless energy. I was only indulging myself by responding to her with male arrogance and was intent on reaffirming myself. In the avalanche of her hair, she cried out intermittently and whispered to me, unable to shape the sounds in her mouth into real words, like a child at midnight. I had misunderstood those whispers completely. I realized that only after I discovered that, carrying out her threats, she had left Japan almost penniless. Her letter in my hand made me aware of my own stupidity. Yet, somewhere in a corner of my heart, I also seemed to welcome the new situation, which rid me of her suffering eyes, her voice, and the weight around my body. Wasn't it the elation of my unburdened heart that made me applaud her braveness? I was certainly more relaxed after this weight had disappeared; and yet I could not stop visiting on my own the places she and I had gone to together where we had spent so many hours joking and talking; I had to reestablish their existence with my own eyes. I wondered if the loneliness I felt was not a mere shadow of my guilt. When something is at hand, it may seem a mere toy; but when it is lost, it suddenly becomes a jewel; one yearns for it. I was absorbed in such childishness. I ate many meals that gave no pleasure to my numbed taste buds, but my heart was still prey to sentiment. The stares and greetings of the waiter who used to wait on us annoyed me intensely; yet when he left the restaurant, I stopped visiting it.

Since that time she has wandered through many countries, and each time she changed her address she sent me a letter. These informed me that she was working as a typist in a Japanese firm, or that she was selling cigarettes in a cabaret; or, after a while, that she had returned to school on a scholarship; she had received a proposal of marriage from a young English atomic scientist; and, again, she was in love with an American linguist of German extraction. Judging from the tone of her letters, she was always indomitable, conscientious, unswervingly driven by curiosity, was constantly moving from one country to another, and was living with great gusto. While in Japan, she railed against the academic cliques that barred her entrance into the field in which she hoped to become a specialist. She complained because publishers would not give her a free hand when she tried to make her way as a translator because they were controlled by the same cliquish scholars, or that she could not advance as she wished when, after a thorough search, she tried her hand as a reporter for the magazine section of a newspaper. She no longer even mentioned all these things that had made her rant and rave every time she saw me while she was still in Japan; she seemed to be excited about the system that accepted her as she was, sometimes clowning, sometimes almost dancing for joy. I weighed each word of every letter.

Meanwhile, I was the victim of undefinable cravings, and traveled abroad thirteen times during the intervening ten years; as soon as I returned, my sole concern was dashing off on another journey. Some of her letters reached me in foreign hotels; after reading them, I tore them to bits as we had formerly promised and scattered the scraps in a river. Invariably either I could not respond to them, being crushed by some other passion, or I was indolent to the point of paralysis. So I could not possibly read these letters in the way she would have me read them. Yet I wrote to her, and wrote words that dulled her affairs with the atomic scientist or the linguist. I am quite aware that I wrote such letters, when I could hardly expect to benefit thereby, out of momentary pangs of jealousy. I was incapable of achieving anything, and I was unqualified for anything; yet I wanted to keep her if I could. The gist of my letters was that she could not possibly settle down to domestic life with any one person because she had known entirely too much freedom. If she were to choose marriage because she could not bear to be lonely, she would be enacting the French proverb that says you can't make an omelet without breaking eggs. But there was also the possibility that the omelet might turn out very badly, and then, unjustifiably, she might curse the egg and feel all the worse as a result. Of course, one never really knows until one has tried several times. I think the reason I wrote something to that effect was that her letters were so light-hearted and vivacious. The only thing I now know was that she had finally gone to a country about which she knew absolutely nothing and had lived there for six years; the university in the capital now accepted her as a visiting staff member of the Oriental Research Department, and she was busy preparing her Ph.D. dissertation for presentation in the fall. And then, beyond the fog of cigarette smoke, I remembered a small scene from long ago. It is night and she is standing, wrapped in her scarlet raincoat, at the entrance to a suburban station, where a ticket collector presents a silent profile. I can see that her rather sharp face was that of someone who had been graduated from college only two or three years before and that, although she looked self-assured, her frightened eyes were not looking at me, but were gazing at something behind my head. A fluorescent light from a small tobacconist shone behind her. A certain expression played on her face, over her high cheekbones; I realize now that it expressed a peace born of resignation, rather than the gentle fatigue that followed love-making. In this far-off scene, I can see her tired, still glittering eyes; I also see the strong lines that run like piano wires through her white, muscular legs—she was once a champion swimmer. Then the scene faded.

It's here; it's time. I left some change beside the mug of grog, bought a ticket from the automatic machine, and walked out to the platform. The train—old, sturdy, green iron boxes that had been made up in a distant northern country and had crossed two more on the way—now approached cautiously, picking its way through the slush on the roadbed, and entered the shadow under the dome. A maze of pale, swollen faces and bleary eyes crowded the windows of the sleeping cars and looked down at me. As I checked one car after another, I walked unawares from the protection of the dome out into the rain, which fell from a dark sky and spattered me relentlessly. I recognized a woman in a scarlet raincoat at the far end of the platform, trying to pull out a suitcase. Just as I started to rush toward her, the downpour began around me in earnest, and the bridge, the cars, the railroad, all disappeared in a black torrent.

She turned around and cried out. Her hair was plastered

over her pale high cheeks, but her eyes shone vividly and her lips were parted. A smile spread over her face.

"You got my telegram."

"Yes!"

"So you came?"

"Of course."

She stood, legs apart, and looked up at me. She held herself erect. Those well-developed shoulders and hips were as strong and sensuous as mountains. Letting the rain beat down on her eyelashes, she said:

"So we meet again, at long last!" She was excited, but under control, and repeated, "So we meet again." She added, "I wonder how long it's been."

"It's been ten years."

"I suppose it has."

"About ten years."

"Yes."

"A lot of water . . ."

She laughed harshly and said: "Yes, under the bridge!"

We passed through the dark, green station and came out onto the square; we decided to go to a restaurant at its edge. Daylight had long since come, but the last traces of night still hovered around the forest of tables with their upturned chairs. A middle-aged bartender in a rumpled white uniform was glumly washing glasses and cups. A young black man was playing the pinball machine in a corner of the empty room. His long, bony fingers and firm hip nudged it, making a thud from time to time. It reverberated with the sound of heavy tools being dropped onto a garage floor.

She ordered coffee with cream and a croissant. I ordered a *pastis.* The ice tinkled in the creamy-yellow liquid and the fresh fragrance of anise softly tickled the tip of my nose. She began to eat her croissant and drink her coffee turn by turn, so I told her that she could break off a piece of her roll and dunk it in the cup. She followed my suggestion docilely and recited her woes: she had been unable to sleep in her berth and had complained to the conductor all night; she had stayed up editing her dissertation to pass the sleepless hours. She seemed to be bursting with excitement to have found someone at last to whom she could complain; but she also seemed to be on the verge of collapsing with fatigue.

Having finished the coffee, she turned the cup upside down on its saucer. In a few seconds she righted it again and examined the coffee grounds that remained in the bottom.

"I'll tell your fortune. I'm very good at it. They rave about it in the seminar. It's not exactly an oracle, but I have a pretty good reputation. Let's see what this is . . . snakes. Three snakes. Three snakes together, wearing glasses. Three bespectacled reptiles. What on earth could this mean?"

"I wonder."

"Wait, I'll tell you."

Suddenly, the rain began to beat down more loudly. We were sitting by a large window on which the prices of hamburgers and sandwiches had been scrawled in white paint. The rain poured against the window, splashed on the pavement, and in no time at all the square was streaming. Station, square, everything disappeared. In the vehement noise of the rain closing in, we were alone, as if on an isolated island.

"It's always raining. Even in summer. It's like this every day where I live too. It's the same wherever you go. I'm really fed up. Every morning when I wake up, I feel as if I'm ten years older."

"It was the same last year. It rained every day. Some papers said it might be an omen of a new Flood. Maybe they meant that we were gradually entering another ice age. It was written in all seriousness and I couldn't really laugh."

"I may be like that. I've grown old. Along with people my age I've survived the grind and competition. Sometimes, though, all of a sudden, I feel totally crushed. It's hard to find oneself collapsing in a foreign country, to feel this alienation. I stay in bed for days at a time doing absolutely nothing. I tell my fortune day by day, by my arms. My arms are strong. In the morning when I wake up, I stretch them, like this, turning them this way and that. Sometimes the blue veins sink deeply into the porcelain white of the fatty tissue and show through its smoothness. On days like that, I feel very encouraged, as if something good might happen. It's more dependable than reading my fortune in coffee grounds. I have relied on my arms for the past ten years."

"You used to say that a long time ago."

"I depended on other things too, in those days, like elbows, shoulders, and legs. I was proud of them. But not any more. I only have my arms to depend on now and I am well aware of it. If I wore a red cap and blue uniform, I'd look like a Salvation Army girl. Sometimes men tease me. I get so angry and I have every intention of fighting back, but then, suddenly I agree with them. I am such a weakling."

"Age has been even harder on me. I don't even have arms to rely on. I'm envious of you. I'm all fat, and I get forgetful, and I have a stiff neck. A real disaster. I take naps from morning to night. I can sleep endlessly. I should try my luck in a competition. I wonder why I'm so sleepy."

"You are sweet to try and make me feel better, but you haven't really changed. I envy you. You should have more self-confidence. Your letters made me think you had become a monster. But I am relieved. You don't seem to have any gray hair either."

"I painted it out with magic ink before coming to meet you."

"I don't like bright places."

"What?"

"I don't want you to see my face."

She spoke softly, quietly. She glanced at me, lowered her eyes, and stretched her hand out to the cigarettes. The spirit that had kept her head high and shone brightly in the spattering rain had disappeared. Maturity weighed on her strong shoulders, and her eyes were sad. She looked as splendid as a ship's figurehead, as she sat with her heavy arms resting easily on the table. But her mouth twitched bitterly at the brim of the coffee cup, something like scars had appeared at the edges of her eyes, something I had never seen before, slight but sharp and irrevocable. I felt as though I were seeing the image of myself as it was reflected in her eyes, and I made her turn away. I saw the shape of my forty years, swollen, still swelling, worn out and flabby, disfigured beyond repair, and bloated with a hangover. If she had been worn down, I had decomposed. The ten years did exist after all. Suddenly, something oppressive rose from each cold, dark corner of the restaurant and overpowered me.

I picked up the glass, listened to the fierce sound of the rain, and sipped one or two drops of cold liquid redolent of anise.

"Is that *ouzo*?"

"Something like that."

"It's a nice drink."

"Good on humid summer evenings."

"I have tasted it in Greece. How long ago was it? I traveled there with some of my departmental students. I think it was near the grave of Agamemnon. At a small drinking place on the roadside. The glass was flyblown. They all had Coke, but I drank *ouzo*."

"Summer?"

"Yes, summer, Greek summer."

"That's nice."

A sudden, bright smile spread over her face, which had been merely sad until then. She leaned forward and stared at me, quickly raising her brows and opening her eyes very wide. Then she gave a swift frown and narrowed her eyes to mere slits. She silently repeated the grimace several times. We broke into soundless laughter.

When we entered the room, she put her suitcase down in one corner and walked around in the scarlet darkness. She turned the doorknob, played with the lock, and turned the bathroom tap on and off; she went around inspecting, with the expert eyes of a seasoned traveler. When she found out that the only luggage I had was the knapsack shoved under the bed, she put both hands on hips and burst out laughing in that young voice. The cocoon filled with fingerprints, nicotine, alcohol stains, and breadcrumbs was shaken vigorously and suddenly changed its appearance, obliterating the prevailing lethargy. At her request I turned off the light. The red gloom vanished and the gray light of early morning streaked through the holes in the curtains and sparkled like powder. After a while, I felt a movement. Turning around, I saw her standing naked. Her thighs, as strong as bridges, shone bronze and blue in the dusky light. She held her voluptuous breasts in crossed arms and covered her face with both hands. She asked timidly, softly:

"Am I still good to look at?"

She was peeping through her fingers.

"Of course. Come."

She ran across in the darkness, jumped into bed, and rolled over with a cry. Her morning body had the coolness and firmness of fruit; her shoulders, breasts, abdomen, thighs knocked and entwined, as lively as small animals. As I tried to bury my face in her opulent breasts, her long arms rose to embrace me passionately. Her warmth radiated through the cold, dewy layer of flesh and pervaded my chest like fresh hot water. I disentangled her arms slowly and rose, kneeling on the bed. I guided her hands to my belt, as we always used to do long ago. She tried to undo the belt, trembling, but had to stop in the midst of her efforts.

"I've been waiting . . . waiting"; moaning, she collapsed.

The rain continued for several more days.

I spent the entire time in my room. The curtains were drawn most of the time, and I did nothing but lounge in bed; she did the shopping. She had learned to speak four languages with ease, but she could not speak this country's language, so I would scribble simple greetings and words for food on a piece of newspaper or notepaper and she would go out with it, walk around in the rain in her flat shoes, and buy everything I had asked for. When she returned she always itemized everything in her small, neat, ant-like writing and placed the list on the edge of the table. The accounting was thoroughly detailed, never missing even the price of a discount subway ticket. I left all the loose money on the table and told her to take as much as she wanted when she went shopping, but she insisted on detailed bookkeeping. Pieces of paper accumulated.

"Don't let that sort of thing bother you."

"Money is money. We must draw a clear line. I'm going to settle the accounts one of these days and make it fifty-fifty; neither of us will owe anything. I don't like to have a falling out because of money. I've been through all sorts of mean business. Really unpleasant experiences. So I can't help worrying. This is love, and that's business. It's better this way and our friendship will last longer. If I depend on you, you'll think I'm adorable to begin with, but sooner or later you will resent it. I know you will; so . . ."

"Forget not thy humility as a beginner, huh?"*

"These are the sad truths I learned as a single woman."

"I'm complimenting your powers of observation and preparation."

"I don't know about that."

She replies with a cheerful smile. Gravely she puts the account on the table; she changes into a negligée and sits up straight in the chair. She looks at me, opening then narrowing her eyes, then suddenly braces herself and plunges into the thick manuscript of the dissertation. She thrusts her fingers into her hair and tousles it; cold intelligence and concentration mark her face. Wielding a ballpoint pen in her left hand like a surgeon's scalpel, she writes rapidly on the manuscript, stopping short at several places. She writes both Japanese and European languages from left to right at breakneck speed. Her swiftness makes me aware of her impressive intelligence.

The room has a curtained window, but it is surrounded by the perpetual dull hum of machinery and sometimes sharp screeches rise over the wave-like sound. The rain beats on the wall and the window and fills the air with the noise of countless small fists secretly knocking. I continually doze and wake up; wake up and doze off. And whenever my skin prickles I invite her to bed. Whenever I call her to bed, she puts down her ballpoint pen as though she were taking off a pair of glasses, gets up from the chair and creeps into bed, hunching her

*Words of Zeami (1363–1443), writer-choreographer who elevated the position of the *Noh* theater to the level of the present art. The major part of the present-day *Noh* repertory is Zeami's work.[*trans.*]

shoulders like a cat. And after responding—committing her entire body—she sometimes chuckles softly and wryly; her pale forehead covered by her long hair, she almost crawls back to the table. . . . Or we get out of bed and plod into the barren bathroom, where a pale light intrudes; we bathe and suck at each other surrounded by patchy concrete walls. When we return to bed, I drink again, make love to her, and sleep; and she makes love, sleeps, and studies. The old, sturdy walls that must have absorbed layer after layer of voices, dirt, and oil never seem to let our voices leak out no matter how loud we shout. They are more like thick, downy flesh than heavy, protective stone. I seem to be inside a cavity protected by the thick membrane of a gigantic, invisible beast with neither form nor face, while at the same time denying all presence. I bury my nose in her armpit and suddenly feel the faint sweet nausea that sometimes attacks me when I am drunk on a smooth wine; I relax into sluggishness, and sprawl as much as I swell. When the scent ripens and my nostrils and face become covered with a sort of dense pollen, I sometimes open the curtains and window. If it happens to be midnight, crisp, dense, blue air flows in, coming perhaps from the cathedral close and the plane-tree-lined promenade on the opposite bank. It is gentle and fresh but also contains a hint of the harsh air of a northern country. It cuts across the bed and the unmoving objects as if it were shaving them with a razor; it scrapes off the multitude of mushrooming things that have spread wherever our fingers touched, and restores everything to its original form; making the rounds of the room, it cleanses even the insides of shoes, and escapes through the window under its own momentum. Swept by this sharp breeze, the crumpled, love-worn sheets suddenly feel laundered and crisply starched, though the wrinkles still remain. The breeze sometimes carries the sound of laughing voices, shattering glasses, and the muffled but insolent threats of wild cats. Perhaps it has wandered through the spacious and coldly empty valley, but the wind bears the imprint of many omens and scars. Sometimes it is streaked with the aroma of freshly baked bread and we are suddenly awakened.

"The town seems to empty out every year," I say.

"It does, doesn't it?"

"I like it. It's nice not to see people. Wherever you go, it's empty, clean, freed of mortal things. It's like the bones of the sperm whale at the zoo. There's no sloppy business."

"You're as misanthropic as ever."

"Very perceptive of you."

"But we're strange. We're camping here. We don't go out to have decent meals, we don't go for a walk, we're living in a cave, like a pair of crayfish."

"We'll go out and splurge one of these days. You can't expect to find a good restaurant at this time of year, but if you look for them, you can find passable ones. I know two or three places. But you must be patient for a little while."

"Why?"

"Good food and sex are not compatible."

"Really?"

"You have to choose one or the other. You can't have them both. Good food is good food; good sex is good sex. You only get sleepy if you indulge in both. They both seem to exist in order to put you to sleep, but I want to know the real taste of each. And then I will go to sleep. So, it's one or the other."

"I don't think you ever mentioned it in those days. Now you seem to be really weakening. You'd better pull yourself together. You were absolutely, ruthlessly irrational in those days. You've changed. I'll pull myself together, too."

"You are right, I was ruthless; or rather, I guess I was.

But I wonder . . . in those days, I probably had raw energy but I didn't know the true flavor of things; maybe I knew nothing about either sensation. I had no way of experiencing either to the point of ultimate exhaustion. There must be a considerable difference between sleeping the sleep of fulfillment and just sleeping without satiation."

"You are playing with sophistry."

"Do you think so?"

"I want to eat chop suey."

"I'll treat you to better things."

"But I *like* chop suey. And as for rice cakes, I like 'persimmon seeds.'* I sent for a five-gallon can full of them the other day from Japan. I went without coffee to save money. As long as I have those rice cakes, I can stand almost anything. No matter what other people are doing, I can be independently happy all by myself. I've brought a bagful. Would you like to see it?"

Her voluptuous breasts bouncing, she drew back from the cast-iron casement and swiftly entered the room. She didn't care if her breasts and pubic hair showed through her thin negligée; she squatted and pulled out a large plastic bag from her suitcase and held it high.

"See, I have all this." She grasped a fistful in her white hand.

"See? I'm independently happy."

She laughed loudly. She rolled into bed, waved her legs like a child, and munched on the crisp rice crackers. She purred like a kitten just given some milk, trying to control her chuckles.

In addition to "persimmon seeds," she had "Master

*Small rice crackers with the flavor of soy sauce and hot pepper, shaped in the form of persimmon seeds. [*trans.*]

Hedgehog," a spongy toy in the shape of a hedgehog, which she used to scrub her body in the bathtub. It seemed to have received a lot of use; the eyes and the nose were worn out, and when its body was squeezed, it gave a grumbling snort as though it were complaining or flurried. She often squeaked it and played with it while she bathed and talked to herself. Before starting work, she always squeaked it once or twice, then opened her notebook or a large dictionary. I knew nothing about the dissertation that she attacked every day except that its content was something that could be named *The Traditional Ambition of Russian Politics in the East, and Its Influence on Asia.* The manuscript into which she seemed to have poured all her energy and attention over several years was filled with neat small writing.

She suddenly raised her face from the notes and asked: "Do you know the expression *ku ai tzu?*"

I answered that I didn't. She wrote three Chinese characters on a piece of paper and quietly slipped into bed. "It's Chinese; they seem to call a parentless child, an orphan, *Ku ai tzu.* Professor Chao in the Research Office told me. Professor Chao is teaching Chinese at the University, but his wife is a calligrapher and they are running a Chinese restaurant on the side. Since I am mad about chop suey, I go there all the time and eat nothing but chop suey. There are chop sueys and chop sueys; if you think all of them are a hash of leftovers, you're wrong. The simpler the dish, the more difficult it is to cook. One night, when I told him my life story while having dinner, Professor Chao wrote the word *ku ai tzu* on a piece of paper and handed it to me over the plate.

"The Chinese are rightly called the men of writing! This word expresses the feeling of helplessness much better than saying 'orphan' or 'parentless child.' I was impressed. It's actually an expression used in an announcement of death by the bereaved child, and it means something like 'an orphan in mourning.' But I am a *Ku ai tzu,* no father, no mother, and I have chosen to desert other relatives. I have one brother, but he changed his name for a particular reason. I like him, but we're so far apart. Besides, I don't intend ever going back to Japan. So, I'm a *Ku ai tzu*— a 'mischief of nature.' " After having spoken, and leaving a trace of warmth behind her in the blanket, she got quietly out of bed. She sat at the table, thrust her fingers through her hair, and squeaked Master Hedgehog with an intense look in her eyes.

She always stopped her work without reluctance. In order to make up for the lost years, or perhaps in order to stop further expansion of the viscous indolence in me, I exhausted all my fervor and improvisation in love-making. We made love in bed, on the floor, in a chair, in the bathtub, from behind, horizontally, sitting, or standing. She and I both felt ashamed about our bodies and preferred darkness to bright light, but as our intimacy grew, we ceased to care. Her flesh, which was exercised by mountain climbing, swimming, and skiing, was exquisitely healthy. When she walked in the nude, even in the red darkness, sharp lines flashed on her thighs and calves. All her limbs were as attractive as in those days many years ago; the only smell was a scent of wholesomeness.

"Do you know a Chinese expression, *kai men hong?*" I asked.

"No, I don't."

"The characters mean Open, Gate, Red. A Chinese immigrant in Saigon taught me. It's used to describe New Year's fêtes and other festivities. It's a word showing the gate wide open, and as you pass by and peep into it, you can see a glimpse of something red, and 'verily, the view is magnificent.' They are indeed a literate people. You can just see it, can't you?"

(23

"It's a clever expression."

"Let's do it and see."

"Turn off the light."

"It'll be Open Gate Black."

"Sorry, can't help it."

A splendid vision opens up right at the tip of my nose. Without lifting my face, I can take in the entire view. I am surprised that this territory bears no trace of the passage of time, and I feel a surge of affection. The sad, clownish, intimate, and yet tauntingly peculiar face of the anus, the wet vagina, its light brown lips parted to the fullest extent, the burst-open appearance of its red protrusion, and the rippling group of small folds, the rustling of warm forests, were all in their characteristic positions. As I lie down in the colossal canyon and lift my face slightly, tickling the wall with my tongue or pecking at it with my lips, I am really gazing into a scene from long ago. She was living alone in those days, in a small building alongside a house surrounded by a low hedge of dusty cypress. The light of an autumn afternoon filtered through the paper screens, shone into every nook and crevice of her white behind held up high. She had met me, in the spring, and she was already miserable by fall. But rather than mention it, she concentrated on telling cheerful jokes. Nevertheless, when she was writhing in ecstasy, her misery oozed out, no matter how she tried to hide it. Her desperate efforts not to give it a definite shape were unsuccessful, and the air of unhappiness unavoidably flooded out. I willfully ignored it, set on pushing the flow of misery from her vagina back into the orifice and imprisoning it there. When she was spent, she fell back on the old felt mattress, crying and panting.

"What's wrong?"

"Don't worry."

Sometimes it was as if misery were running out like pus

from various parts of her magnificent body. Such a shadow of unhappiness sometimes appeared accidentally long before she became depressed; but I was overwhelmed by all the signs of misfortune that appeared later, and made the mistake of thinking that the early trend foretold them all. Much later, after she left for abroad, while I reminisced about us and went over the details, I began to feel that perhaps her misery existed before her unhappiness, in her very backbone. I began to think that perhaps her depression was secreted from her spinal column, out of her past. I was often told that she was an orphan. She had told me many times about her mother, father, brother, her childhood, and girlhood. But as I followed her autobiography and the episodes that escaped her lips, there was a considerable blank in her story after a certain point in her girlhood. It was missing completely. What this *ku ai tzu* did alone during that time, and where and how she earned a living, I did not know at all. Misery was probably a heritage from that time, becoming as much a part of her as a body odor, and no matter how she suppressed it, it continued to flow within her. I, too, was still saturated with the misery and shame of my boyhood and could not escape from the shadow of its huge hand. In those days in Japan, if a girl not much younger than I had to wander about the asphalt jungle as a *ku ai tzu,* I think I could guess what she did and did not have to do, to survive. She was probably saved by some experience so fragile that it might have collapsed instantaneously and completely at the slightest touch. She probably could do nothing but be silent and patient. Behind the impulse that drove her from Japan, there was, of course, her hatred of the academic cliques and the hopelessness of marriage to me, but I wonder if there was not also a vague but persistent emanation from her unmentionable past that kept rising to the surface like methane: She seemed to be keeping a diary every day, not in Japanese but in the language of the country where she is living now. I was secretly astonished by this, but perhaps something of the sort was necessary for her.

Her spectacular behind trembles. Small drops of perspiration stream down her thighs, turn to mist and disappear. Her bottom is held higher and higher in the red darkness. Her thighs quiver, go loose, and her genitals descend. My nose and mouth are buried in warm liquid, which overflows and drops from my chin.

"There, there, more," she moans.

"Like this?"

"Yes. More, more.

"Try to wrap your tongue around it."

"Like this?"

"Scream! Yell! In Japanese!"

"Impossible. That's too much. Don't tell me to shout when I have such a mouthful. One of the two. It's got to be one or the other. Just one. There. Ah!"

Suddenly my face is covered with wet flesh, and I am shoved away; my head bumps into the headboard with a big thump. A long, lonely, full-throated groan soars in the red darkness, and her weight, which had been supported by her stomach and back muscles, falls on me in its entirety. The sheet is as hot as a furnace. She covers me, swaying like a ship that has taken on a bellyful of cargo, and, quivering with overwhelming rhythmic sensations, sinks soundlessly down into lower and still lower depths through the floor of the room, onto the railroad bed of the subway, all the way to the depths of the earth where one strikes oil.

The hot tap in the bathroom sometimes worked, other times not. Sometimes the water was hot, sometimes lukewarm. It was so capricious that we never knew which would come until we turned on the tap each day. If she finds out that the hot water is running, she takes off all her clothes and rushes into the bathroom. She fills the big, blotchy old bathtub with hot water and squeezes the Badedas tube; the green liquid drips out. As soon as it touches the hot water, it turns into white foam and swells like cotton candy. She has brought the bubble bath with her and it is pleasant. You don't have to scrub and polish your body. Just by soaking in it, you are cleansed by the foam. If the froth dissolves, all you have to do is add some more liquid. You don't have to dry your body when you get out of the tub. I am immersed in lukewarm water, buried in the foam up to my chin; holding a thin cigar in my right hand and a glass of vodka in my left, I read a newspaper that is propped against the wall. I watch her play with the hedgehog.

"The cigar tastes good like this."

"Yes?"

"I wonder why."

"I wonder."

"The smoke gets moistened by the hot water."

"Smoking a cigar in a bathtub is what big gangsters do, isn't it? You see a lot of that in the movies. Edward G. Robinson, for instance. There was a film called *Key Largo* some years back. He is in a bathtub, looking like a chronic liver or kidney patient, a cigar hanging from his mouth, and he calls a henchman and gives orders in his husky voice."

"It's not only gangster bosses; critics do that too. Whisky in his right hand and a cigar in his mouth, a newly published book in his left hand that he scans from the corner of his eye. He scribbles something, slowly, delicately. Sometimes he writes like a prophet, sometimes like a victim of something, and often in a mixture of both. I hear they are called 'bathtub critics.' The writers may be doing the same thing, it's quite possible."

She is fond of energetic hot baths; she likes the fresh bite, the piercing shock of the water. She knows that, if she crouches there, holding her knees, her blood will soon start to pound, and she can enjoy watching the sensational transformation in her own body. As a matter of fact, as she suddenly stands up from the foam, the drops of hot water roll down her voluptuous white body, stream down the mountains and fields and forests in a roar, and then from underneath, a body of magnificent pink porcelain, glistening all over, appears through the soft, hazy screen. From the deepest core of white flesh, her entire body shines as if lit by a soft lantern, as if it had triumphed over the barren walls, the spotty bathtub, and the cracked mirror.

She goes into the room completely nude, covered with white foam, and looks around in the red darkness thick with the odor of cigars and perspiration; discovering that there is nowhere else, she jumps up on the bed.

"Look, look!" she laughs cheerfully. Flashing her legs and exposing her navel, pubic hair, and entire genital area, she jumps up and down.

"See, I'm Coppelia!" she cries out.

"Look! The Sleeping Beauty!" And in a kind of chant, "There! The Swan!" she laughs. "I'm too good to become a Ph.D.!"

In moments like this, her face is open and alive, and her

small white teeth shine; her eyes flare with a fierce, provocative, dauntless brilliance.

While scrubbing the expanse of her strong back covered with white foam, I smoke a cheap cigar, and gaze rapturously into the snow-lantern glow that shines from her core after each stroke. Her skin, without the down, coarse hair, and pores of a white woman, is smooth, dewy, and velvety like white satin, and it does not seem to suffer from sleepless nights, or the heat of the sun, or prodigious work. In spite of abuse after abuse, her skin seems to revive each morning from the ashes and shows no sign of deterioration. Looking at the light flickering on the dense flesh of her shoulder under the trembling foam, I say:

"Your ancestor seems to have gone astray. Rather recently, too. Your father, mother, grandfather, or grandmother, someone like that. Haven't you heard anything about it? There was someone who had an affair with a Caucasian."

"There might have been someone."

"Asian skin is smooth. Both men and women. Korean women especially are rare treasures. They are almost uncanny. Only they don't have enough fat. Caucasian women have white skin, but it's like chalk. Coarse, rough, and porous. Their insides would leak right through if it weren't for the considerable amount of fat they have; that makes up for it. If an Asian woman's skin had a Caucasian's fat, it would be fine. Yours seems to have achieved that ideal combination."

"You talk like a Persian slave merchant. You slept around while I wasn't looking, didn't you? You are assessing me. You are scrutinizing me meanly. You look at me as though you were studying a terra cotta or a vase of the Yi dynasty, like an 'object.' I know."

"But you seem to be full of confidence."

She chuckles softly and immerses herself in the foam. The

(29

great luminous lantern slowly submerges in the hot water, a blend of green and white. A number of slow whirlpools form around her shoulders and then disappear.

When I enter the warm chamber of the vagina and stay in the darkness, I feel sometimes a surge of sweet, melting nausea. I fight against it, and in spite of myself I try to read the passage of time in the trembling movements of her folds. I try to detect her past by touch. I try to find traces of the work of at least two men who must have passed this way. Shortly after entering the chamber, on the right-hand side there used to be a soft, small, flexible object that was like a bird's beak. I muster all my senses to see whether it has shrunk or enlarged. I advance little by little, listening to every movement. This is not jealousy. Rather, it springs from a vague feeling something akin to friendship. The nub is still there. I stop. It's still there. It welcomes me and rises sensitively and softly; delicately and quickly it starts to nudge me, to recede, and to tremble. Could it be called Cupid's arrow? It is like the lively dance of a dwarf. It has not changed. Nothing has changed. Nostalgia rises and slowly spreads wide. Behind my shoulders, I sense the sliding paper windows where the afternoon sun is shining. Beyond the window is a dusty cypress hedge. There are muffled voices in the distance.

Laying my temple on the hot thigh of the woman who has just come out of the bathtub, I look at the hair tipped with shining bubbles. Satiated and fatigued, I playfully concentrate on trying to arouse the small bud that is hidden in the fuzz, using my tongue and lips. Lazily I look at her bottom and at the path, not hidden in the usual darkness but rudely illuminated by an unusual brilliance in every fold and corner. Finally, becoming aware of the light, I raise my eyes and find the window and the bed at eye level. I did not realize that the curtains had been opened; the mercurial sunset so characteristic of northern countries is aglow. Red, purple, navy blue—every color is shining faintly and serenely, and the edges of the hazy clouds, stitched by silvery thread, sparkle. The window is shining, the dictionary is shining, the room is shining. The light has completely invaded her hair and on each minute fold of the wet, brownish lips, a crystalline liquid glistens. I stretch my hand out on the table and look at my watch. It is eight o'clock. Eight in the evening.

I bury my nose and say: "The rain seems to have stopped."

The back street is like a valley, and a gutter also. It is narrow and dark, and the walls are soaked in rain; urine, feces, and garbage are scattered everywhere. The area is inhabited by exiles and emigrants from various countries, and poor eating places and barber shops stand with darkened windows; cobblestones, walls, windows, all give off acrid, viscous smells of oozing, sweating matter. Graffiti are everywhere: "Fuck you!"; "Monkey"; "Workers and students, unite!"; "Up with violence and rape!"; "No!"; "Do it!" I walk slowly through this dark gutter swarming with hidden life and filled with a choking, sour odor, and I come out onto a boulevard. Suddenly the sunlight floods everything; the summer has recovered from its sickness and everything is shining like a northern lake: the sky, the cathedral, the plane tree-lined promenade, and the walls on the banks of the river. The sun lights up my body too, bathing every corner of it, and I am filled with a clear, rarefied light. When I was walking through the gutter, my body was sprinkled with the warm pollen of her body, her breath, and her whisper, and they barely sustained me in my exhaustion. But now everything has evaporated in the moment the sun struck me. Everything is hazy and dazzling. There is neither sound nor sweat.

"I feel like a sick man, drifting."

"Shall I take your arm?"

"No, don't. I'll walk."

She mutters something and chuckles quietly. There are no black circles under her eyes, no bags. Only the wry smile of indomitable maturity.

As we climb up the gradual slope of the boulevard, the large show windows shine red and gold and black. The pavement is congested: noisy, long-haired students selling political underground newspapers; the barrel organ mumbling like slowly dripping water; the precise lazy answers of waiters; the eyes of young women who can size up the situation at a glance; the nicotine-stained goatees of professors. At the edge of the pavement sits an old man. He has a circle chalked on the road, and a tin box for coins. An unwrapped bottle of Napoleon Cognac stands on one side of the box. He takes out five worn cardboard disks and throws them one by one.

"Look!"

"Like this!"

"There, there!" Calling out to no one in particular, he throws the disks perfunctorily. Each disk flies and falls within the chalked ring, forming a circle with the other disks, none of them overlapping even one millimeter. When all five disks fall, they look like a precise geometric figure. Students pass by and try their hand at it, but the second or third disk always overlaps. The old man, with a twitching smile on his amiable face, politely picks up coins from the students' hands and drops them in the change box with a clinking sound.

"Is that all?"

"That's all."

"You mean, if you can arrange the disks in that circle without overlapping, you get the bottle?"

"Right."

"You're just out of liquor. Shall I get it for you? I've been very good at this sort of thing ever since I was a child. I used to play havoc on fairgrounds. Shooting stalls, catching goldfish, I was a crackerjack. I always beat my brother and pleased my mother. That hedgehog I have now—my toy box was always full of prizes like that. Do you have some change?"

"Only three tries. All right?"

"You're stingy."

She squatted on the roadside and received the disks from the old man, and after exercising her fingers, aimed carefully and threw them. The first time, the second disk overlapped the first. The second time, the third disk overlapped. The third time, also, the third overlapped. The old man showed his twitching smile, and furtively picked up three coins from the vexed girl and dropped them in the change box. The box was already full of coins and nearly overflowed.

"Isn't he playing some sort of trick?"

"No tricks."

"I feel as though I've been cheated."

"That is the art of a great master."

A little farther on a small, middle-aged man and a young woman stood surrounded by a crowd of students. The small man had a bald head shaped like an irregular egg, and he looked shabby but neat; his eyes serious, he was delivering a speech. But the minute he began to speak, all the students taunted and jeered him. He was not at all abashed no matter how much he was taunted, berated, or mocked; but because the students' delighted shouts were so loud, he was unable to proceed with his speech and he just stood there with annoyance in his small, clear eyes. The young woman became excited and climbed up the iron fence; hanging onto a bar by one hand, she began to rail against the students in sharp, passionate tones. The students grew more boisterous than ever. The woman turned her head to follow the voices if they came from the right, and turned to the left if the jeers flew from that side; eyes flaring, mouth grimacing, she started to argue every student into silence, as if protecting the small man who was at a loss.

"What is going on?"

"I don't understand too well. But he's an electrical engineer and writes poetry too. And he's making a speech to the effect that a man should have three years of rest for every year of work. He says that that is what's called an ideal society. He's saying that we must build such a society, and if he is elected he'll start such a movement. She may be his supporter or she may be his secretary. She may be a comrade. Sometimes she even looks as if she might be his daughter. Every day they come out like this and let the students make fun of them. But no matter how much they are teased, they don't seem to be discouraged. They are serious. They're not crazy. You might really call them 'voices in the wilderness.' Anyway, there are lots of eccentrics in this neighborhood."

"I'm all for working one year and doing nothing for three, if someone lets me. Isn't that a nice policy? I'll vote for them without any question. There's no reason to tease them like that."

"Then why don't you tell them that you agree."

"Tell me how to say it."

Suddenly she shouted the words she learned from me, twice, loud and clear. The woman who was hanging onto the iron fence heard it and turned her face towards us. Her eyes, which had been shining like a panther's, suddenly narrowed

in a smile, and her head nodded. Then she turn
neck toward the students again and started to

We went to the park and sat on our bench
vendor, an old woman selling pigeon food, a balloon ve
a cotton candy vendor, all worked in the hazy evening sun,
which flashed like mercury; they called out to the pedestrians
who walked past in groups. The frog man was also working
hard. Today he had three frogs in the goldfish bowl. The rain
had gone on for many days, and he had probably waited
patiently in his garret, taking good care of his frogs; expecting
a big crowd today, he had probably come out with a lot of
water in the jar. He stopped on the roadside and opened his
mouth wide, hung out his tongue limply, slowly swallowed his
frog, and with a roll of the eyes, calmly and gravely hit his
gigantic stomach. The water gushed out like a pump and out
jumped the frog. The man took the coins handed over by the
glazed-looking spectators, and retreated to the shade of a tree,
holding his goldfish bowl and jar, to lie down. The spectators
left; after a while, when he saw new pedestrians approach, he
would rise slowly, gulp down some water, and go out into the
road.

"Isn't he a deaf-mute?"

"No. I've seen him talking at a bar. He's no mute. He
was doing the same thing last year, and three years ago, too.
Every time I come here I make a point of coming here to see
if he's still here. I feel relieved when I see him. He's completely disdainful of everything. It's refreshing. Lao-tzu would
have been delighted to see him. Sloth is the True Way."

"It's rather grotesque, don't you think?"

"It's not easy to be that thorough and lazy at the same
time. I like that. I might as well say I'm impressed. During the
war, when everybody was careening about in a flurry of panic,

was probably silent, alone, and swallowing and spitting out
frogs. I like to think so. It's not easy to reach nirvana to that
degree. He is a spiritual dandy. 'Studied casualness' is a term
for foppery, I hear; he really has that. What do you think?''

"I quite understand what you are trying to say. But to me
he's an Oblomov. That's right. He's an Oblomov swallowing
and spitting out a frog. Oblomov is in and out of bed all day,
just talking. But this man has come out on the street and begun
to swallow and spit out the frog. Some great philosopher has
said that an intellectual is someone who creeps into bed and
chokes on his own wind, called self-reflection. This one's
choking on a frog. The difference is only between the frog and
wind, isn't it? You say Lao-tzu would be pleased. I say Ionesco
or Beckett would be delighted.''

"No, Lao-tzu. Look at him. He has no air of tragedy. He's
content. The theater of the absurd has none of his style. The
laughter of the absurd is sophisticated but it's convulsive.
There's no abandonment. It is a sudden attack. I'd rather take
this man, if I had my way. As a matter of fact, I've been
thinking he might be used in something, a novel or a play. But
I haven't had a good idea for it. Whether I should use him in
the main role, or in a secondary role, or as a man who moves
the plot, I have no idea. So, I just stand and watch him.''

"Well, that may be impossible.''

"Why?''

"Because that's a perfect art in its own way. Anything
perfect is unassailable. So you can't adapt it. Leave him alone.
That is the art of a true master.''

She squinted in the evening sun, and, suddenly, her
breasts shook and she burst out laughing. At that moment, the
man, who had entertained a group of spectators and sent them
off, had just swallowed some water in a particularly grave
manner and spat out the frog, though no one was now watch-

(36

ing him. He picked up the jumping frog and washed it in the fishbowl affectionately, then he held the water jar under his arm, and slowly walked out of the park. The clear sunlight sparkled, and dark spots of water remained on the sandy road.

It is customary for me to spend the hours before evening in the cheap bar at the foot of the bridge. The chairs covered with woven vinyl cords in red, yellow, and black are left on the pavement. I sit leaning on the back of one of them, and sip a martini, taking my time. The hours that are neither day nor night give me a vague expectation of something new and exciting; I feel it in the glass, in the ashtrays, and in the rustling of the promenade trees. As I pick up the dry-martini glass, which is covered by minute drops of condensation, it has the solid weight of a gem; I roll a freezing cold drop on my lip, and a faint, fresh bitterness surrounds the hard core; the chill of the liquid is vivid, dark and clear all the way to its center. The hazy, cheery evening passes slowly, and soon, the night steals in like water, from the road, trees, lights, and voices, spreading to cover the boulevard; soon, before I'm aware of it, it is riding overhead, soaking the awning, invading the windows, irradiating the roofs, and filling the sky with a tender chill. Immediately before that, there is a momentary period when a clear but violent brilliance—red and violet— fills the air. It is a mere second or two. By the time one notices it and starts to pay attention, it is already gone. It is at such a time that one realizes that the austerity and the white harshness of the day exist only for these moments. The boulevard is filled with the gleam of blood, everything is saturated with a dark brilliance; paper trash, statues, broken bits of refuse, buildings, her fingernails, her breasts, all surge with a secret rhythm. When evening comes in the warm countries, chaotic energy reverberates and explodes, but its steaming abundance depresses one . . . I have never witnessed so clearly defined a moment of passion. The boulevard is now a pandemonium of confusion and shouts. Her face, neck, and hair are drenched in violet light, which gives them a totally unfamiliar touch of pathos and dignity. As I try to sit up, it's already gone. Under the bright light, it is the girl student in her thirties smiling, and showing her small teeth.

"Shall I light it for you?"

"No, thank you."

I put my hand in my pocket and located the Zippo lighter and lit a cigarette. The turmoil had gone; night had clearly fallen. The witching hour had passed. Magic came alive, danced in the streets, played around the newspaper stalls, stole up to bar counters and seduced people; but after invoking all its powers, it evaporated without binding anything in its spell, vanishing as though all the applause had faded.

"The evening newspaper boy was here," she said.

"I didn't notice."

"I thought he was here and shouted something; then the next moment he was gone. It's too much, isn't it? Though they do have to be very quick, he's like a bat. Shall I chase him and get a copy? Do you have something to read tonight?"

"I don't care about the papers. On the other hand, pots of food must be cooking in restaurants. Think about it and decide where you want to go and what you want to eat. You're always studying. Maybe you have no appetite, but you can't live on 'persimmon seeds' and chop suey. It's been like a camping trip for some time."

"I've no idea. Anyway, where I live now is potato and sausage country. Just try living there for ten years. You'll become parsimonious, sturdy, earnest, and hard working. Your taste buds grow quite senile and you can't do a thing about it. You might as well decide for me; I'll follow you to the ends of the earth. I'll eat anything. I know I'll be safe with you. If I follow you, I'll get good food. We must not scorn our sensuous pleasures! Take me anywhere, to a bathhouse, or an opium den . . . anything!"

"Don't be sarcastic. I'm talking about eating. The question is what we will eat tonight. How would you like 'innards'? They're good. I know a good place on Filth Alley. When you sit down, the waiter comes with a telescope and lets you peep at the menu on the door. What today's special is depends on the day. But in general, it is some sort of innards, cooked in wine and spices for hours and hours. It is served in a small pot. Heart, liver, stomach, intestines, testicles, kidneys, you don't know what will be served, but everything's good. Take kidneys, for instance. Rather than being completely cleaned and bloodless, it's better when a trace of urine is still there; they have more bite to them. There are paintings that come alive because of one casual faulty stroke in a thoroughly self-conscious, calculated work. It's the same thing. Kidneys should have a little smell of urine, a trace of it."

"How about testicles?"

"You don't understand! You must learn more about the facts of life. The testicles have nothing to do with urine. But they're not bad. They're spongy, rubbery, and very subtle. I ate some fried calf's testicles in a Madrid slum bar, with sangría. It was a truly refined and pure taste, soft and round; without being told I wouldn't have known what it was, but even after I knew I couldn't believe it. They had the texture of the steamed white fish served at an elegant tea ceremony dinner. In general, intestine dishes are not to be slighted. Fish, animals, anything, if they kill an enemy, they will eat the intestines before anything else. How about it tonight? The hors d'oeuvre should be snails. Not the canned ones, but fresh ones. These people here go to graveyards and if they see snails around the gravestones they get excited; they say this is big, this is small, and they fight for them to take home. They cry with the right eye and eat with the left.''

"Wonderful attitude! I approve! Their ancestors will be pleased. I'm getting hungry. I'm glad I wasn't careless to mention chop suey. It was a close call. Let's go, now! To Filth Alley.''

Laughing, she wrinkled the corners of her eyes and stood up from the chair. She pushed back the sleeves of the tartan-checked sport shirt a little and pretended she was ready for a battle. Her arms were taut and muscular, with an underlay of gleaming blue-white. They shone like bronze in the night that was trying to invade the restaurant, having swallowed up the boulevard and awning, and yet the night stopped and hesitated.

The restaurant in the back road is poor, small, and absolutely filthy. The tables and walls seem to be painted with a coat of their customers' dirt and grease nearly one centimeter thick. It is as dark as a cave, but a small, round spotlight shines on the door. A crudely printed menu is pasted on it. When a customer comes in, the waiter brings a telescope without a word. It is a shabby old object from the pirate ages, and the paint is peeling off all over it.

"I see it; I see the slaughterhouse!" She raises her voice.

"Just pretend you are looking."

The old proprietor of the restaurant, as thin as a blade, comes up and I order bread, wine, snails, and the day's special. They don't use snail shells here, but a small, toy-like pot. Little by little you fill your plate with the golden foaming butter from the pot, which exudes a delicious garlic fragrance as you eat the snails and soak up the sauce with the bread. Finally, you wipe the plate with a piece of bread and soak up the butter completely. The delicious burning odor of the breadcrust, garlic, butter, and the snail fat remains on your tongue. You wash it all down with a glass of wine.

"I'll teach you. You'd better remember this. This is true of any alcoholic drink. As you take it in your mouth, you swill it over your gums and let it soak. And wait a little until the true nature of the wine develops, then examine it. Your gums are important. If you watch a real connoisseur drink *saké,* you'll notice that his cheek suddenly swells like a balloon. That's what he's doing. They say this is 'biting into wine.' Actually I've never tasted such a high-grade *saké* that I want to bite, so I always gulp it down with just my tongue and throat as though I were gargling. Good bread is another thing. That's all you need to enjoy wine."

"What innards are they serving today?"

"I don't know. You just eat whatever they serve. The best thing to do when you come to this sort of place is to leave it to the restaurant."

"You can tell by the smell. Right?"

"Shall I ask them to make it stronger?"

"No. I'm only joking."

Soon the pots of food appear, steaming hot. With a fork I pick out a tender, limp object and put it on the plate. It is stomach. It is well stewed, tender and meaty, but some resiliency is still there and you can enjoy biting into it. The rich, thick sauce has permeated it completely, and its smoothness is more that of perfect ripeness than of cooking. It is like a ripe, juicy fruit. To begin with she exclaimed, "Delicious! Wonderful!" but soon fell silent. She picked the stomach from the pot and put it on the plate, tore off the bread, sometimes rested her hand and sipped wine, then sighed and returned to work.

Wiping all the sauce on the plate with a piece of bread

and swallowing the last bit, she sank back into the chair as if exhausted, and leaned against the wall. She was perspiring faintly and her cheeks were flushed; her eyes had a vacant glaze and shone in the darkness.

"Perfect!" she moaned. "Inexpressibly perfect. I feel quite soporific. You were right about good food making one feel dazed."

Shyly, she stroked her stomach lightly and smiled. Her eyes were shining but vacant, smokily glazed; they had the same expression when she slipped out of a man's arms covered in perspiration. If satisfaction spells euphoria, it is small wonder that gourmandise and sex show the same face. Intoxication is like a gentle hill glistening under the life-giving sun; the scent of grass rises bountifully and lingers with the same sweetness even after the zenith of the day. This is even more like sex. But why is it that no residual hint of cold arrogance lingers around the corners of her mouth when she is obviously seeking pleasure solely in order to satisfy her desire?

Suddenly she sits up straight.

"Let's stay here for several days, then travel to my home. I'll give you a treat this time. I'll bake a pizza. It's not an ordinary sort of pizza. I start from scratch, with yeast and flour, and I knead the dough. I leave it for hours and hours and let it rise, then the real work begins. Anchovy, salami, olives, I use everything I can think of. What do you call them, those small green berries pickled in brine? I buy a jar of them and stud the pizza with them. I'll use plenty of everything, since you're so hard to please. My pizzas are famous in the department. I put up a notice on the bulletin board announcing that I'm going to bake pizza on such and such a date. And, then, ah, *everybody* shows up! From Oriental studies, Slavic studies, old professors, young professors, the assistants, they come in droves. Some of them ask, 'When will you have the next pizza party?' while they're still eating. So you see, real ability is at work here. It's exactly what I advocate. Only the real action counts. Besides, where I'm staying now is like a castle of glass and steel. It's an oblong box. An academic foundation built it as scholars' sleeping quarters, but it's quite impressive. You can adjust the humidity, dryness, temperature, anything, with a thermostat dial. Of course, you can open the huge glass door with a touch of the hand so you can go out on the balcony if it's warm in the evening. I'll buy a deck chair so you can lie down on it with only a pair of shorts on. You are always ready to take off your clothes, aren't you? But the strange thing is that you hear crickets singing when you are in the bathtub— in this ultra-modern, three-storied building; at first I thought it might have been my hedgehog. But it wasn't. It's crickets. They climb up the pipe. Always two of them, saying 'Long time no see.' They're adorable; so I named them. The one that looks stronger is Hans, and the quiet one is Inge. Strangely, they come out only at night, and only when I'm in the bathtub. They sing so helplessly, so sadly. You might describe it as a violin played by a lonely woman. I want you to meet them; I think you'll like them.''

"What can you cook beside pizza?"

"How about *cha ts'ai mien*? I'll go to Professor Chao's restaurant and ask Madame Chao to let me have pressed vege- tables and noodles. I might even take a thermos jar and ask for some soup, too. I don't know whether your taste buds will approve of it, spoiled as you are in Southeast Asia, but let's try it anyway. Madame Chao is a master calligrapher, but she's very unpretentious and shouts '*Aiya*!' every so often. They say she's very capable. The amazing thing is that the two of them came with only one suitcase between them, and in three years they have a restaurant. Oh, yes, besides the pressed vegetables and noodles, I can cook chop suey, a recipe straight

(43

from Madame Chao. Don't laugh. You look like saying, 'Again?' But you try it and then criticize. Mushrooms are in season now and I'll use them; a lot of them."

"I have a favor to ask of you."

"What is it?"

"Do it as if you're playing with a doll's house."

I spoke, then fell silent, and lit my cigarette. She did not seem to notice my agitation. She had folded her arms under her high, jutting breasts, and with her head slightly tilted, she was euphorically, openly, smiling. I want her to play this as a game: pizza, deck chair, the noodles, chop suey, everything. If possible, I don't want her to make it either more or less than that. Otherwise, it will be devastating. We'll be repeating the same mistake again. I started to say this, but remained silent.

Her lingering expression might have been induced by the wine and rich food; nonetheless, as her face floated in the cavernous darkness lit by candlelight, I saw an elation and a deep content that I had never seen in the past. The halo that shone and radiated around her seemed to come from the deep and distant past, over many years and months. I could not hope to detect its source. She seemed happy. Filtering through the struggles and loneliness was an air of serenity. She was narrowing her eyes, and her entire body radiated it; yet she was not aware of it. She cocked her head; was she already trying to listen to the two crickets? I couldn't believe that happiness could possibly be so prodigal. I felt a little insecure, suffocated.

On our return to the inn, we walk through a back street. It is noisy for a while in the evenings, but it is already a black gutter again. There is no one around. Here and there, the lights from bars and restaurants light up the entrances like cavities, but our footsteps echo faintly against the walls. We feel as though we are immersing ourselves in dirty water as we enter the darkness of the alley. These are mounds of rocks that, we begin to suspect, have never seen the light of day ever since they were carried down from the mountains when the city was first founded. They have been frozen ever since they absorbed winter. As we pass these wet, stubborn walls, I suddenly catch a whiff of the warm fragrance of flowers in the midst of the chokingly acrid odor of urine. I stop in the darkness.

"I wonder if someone just passed by?"

"I don't know."

"Did you hear footsteps?"

"We have been alone all along."

"You didn't hear a door closing, did you?"

"I don't think so."

"But I do smell perfume. It's not yours. I just caught a whiff. It was as though I had walked past a woman, fresh and eager. It's mysterious because no one seems to be here. I wonder why."

"Do you want to make love to a ghost?"

Chuckling in a low voice, she suddenly entwined her arm in mine and pulled me over; standing on tiptoe, she offered me her lips.

In about a week we moved.

She took her raincoat and suitcase in her hand and I carried a knapsack on my back. We went to the station and got into the train after buying bread, wine, and ham at the grocery store in the square. The compartment was full of migrant workers.

They were small but muscular, and their skin looked

(45

dusky, as if they had been smoked, and their eyebrows were dark. They came from the poor villages and slums of the south, and they were about to go to the rich north to mix cement on the construction sites or to boil asphalt on the roadside. The women would wash dishes at restaurants or would clean buildings and railroad stations. The trains coming down from the north smelled of flowers and those ascending smelled of sweat. The passengers chattered loudly and shouted, and their many quick gestures were brash and unbridled. Once their companions left them, however, the men's eyes grew suddenly lonely and the women fell pathetically solemn. Men savored their cigarettes, smoking them all the way down until they burned their nails. At noon, one after another they took from their string bags salami with plenty of garlic and pepper, dill pickles, and cherries and offered some to us, and politely drank the wine that we offered to them. They would connect bits of words and phrases that they must have scraped from the roadsides and railroad stations of various countries to comment, "It's wonderful"; "It's good for your health"; or "It's a real drink for men."

Summer was finally ripening. The signs of an approaching flood and ice age had temporarily disappeared, and a hazy but warm and expansive sun flooded the area. The wheat was a dazzle of gold in the fields, the forests were heroically dark; camping vehicles and tents fought for ground by the lake, and fat, white bodies exhausted with eating lazed there or bathed in the water. Sluggish cows on the oceans of richly undulating hills hung their heads. As the train moved slowly up into the mountains, we could see clear, blue water cascading down under sharp precipices, splashing white foam from one rock to another, in the black shadows of the forests.

My eyes moved from the rocks to the forests, from the forests to the water, from the water to the mountain ridges, and I wondered about the age of this area; I appreciated its purity, and was totally captivated by the signs of solitude that stood all around. Each time I saw deep gorges and shallow streams, pools, falls, and whirlpools, my eyes forced me to stop and wonder and ponder on where and how I should throw my hook and how I should let it drift. The scenes of blood and devastation receded and became nothing but a dull pain like a toothache; I put my face against the window and, sipping wine in the sparkling sunshine, kept thinking about sharp fishing hooks, the hard, white mouth of a trout, the fat, but solidly resilient flash that would feel resistant to my fingers, and the spots that were like powdered gemstones glistening in the sunshine, and I never got bored on the trip.

When visiting a city one has never seen, it's better to arrive at night. One can see only what is lamplit; it's like entering a city wearing a mask, like peeping at things through a hole; the eyes concentrate only on what the darkness has condensed for us. The morning after, when the ruthless and merciless sun exposes whatever banality, mediocrity, poverty, and misery exist, it is better than having encountered them for the first time in broad daylight. At least one can be surprised by the total change since the night before, or be disappointed, or sometimes even made to chuckle. Regardless of whether one arrives in daylight or at night, ennui will sooner or later catch up. Therefore, it is better to choose an arrival that has some element of surprise, even just a little. One's vision is as acute as one's sense of smell, but it gets accustomed to things rather fast and becomes placid, thus only helping to kill passion. If this is so, one should at least preserve one moment of shock and enjoy the effect of the 180-degree reverse of night and day, so that one can jeer at oneself by taking a step backwards. Hence my decision: I told her to get a timetable and arrange trains so that we would arrive at our destination late at night, even though it meant that we would have two transfers and a wait, and inconvenience all around.

"This is not your first visit, is it?"

"That's right. I've been to the area twice, to a couple of cities, but I have never been here. I don't know anything about it. I want you to take me around as though you were leading a blind man by the hand."

"I understand. Leave it to me. I even know the rat holes. I won't let you down. Ask me anything. Now it's my turn to take over. Let's go."

"It's too quiet for a capital city."

"Of course. Here we have only government offices and universities. It's not like Tokyo. Besides, the natives all go home at nine at night and the whole town goes to bed. I live in the suburbs a little further away. We can hear owls hooting even during the day."

"Do owls hoot during the day?"

"Yes, and they read philosophy books at night."

"Never heard of such a thing before."

"That's why they suffer from insomnia."

We had been sitting for a long time, and, here and there, muscles and bones protested. Disregarding the pain, I carried the knapsack on my shoulders and got off the train onto the platform. A mere handful of shadowy figures got out with us; all around, cool deep night had suddenly fallen, only occasionally punctuated with pale-blue holes of fluorescent light. The usual shouts, laughter, twinkling eyes, flashing teeth, and the vague but gigantic rumbles that one finds at any train station of any capital city were nowhere to be found here. She was excited; her shoulders held high, she marched majestically through the dark underpass, which echoed to the click of her high heels.

She said that a trolley was still running and she wanted

to use it; I insisted on taking a taxi. We loaded the noble tank-like car, a Mercedes, with our luggage. After giving the driver the destination, rapidly and fluently, she sank back into the leather seat and analyzed in detail the difference in price between a trolley and taxi in serious, reproachful tones, continuing to claim emphatically that this was a nonsensical luxury and that she would never have committed such folly. Her voice had changed completely. Previously she had been restrained, and even if she sometimes became bold, she was always pliable and modest, minimizing herself by her voice or by glancing out of the corner of her eyes. Suddenly she had loosened up, thickened, gained confidence, and she was trying to protect me from behind. Although she was still gentle and quiet, she was about to spread her great wings with solid determination. I concentrated on looking out at the deep night in this busy and ascetic capital city, now contracted by darkness. There were a number of squares, and the promenades let the muscular shadows cast by the lower branches of trees lie across the pavement; neon signs were declaiming silently. Clear lights were shining in bars, restaurants, and dress shops, but no human shadows were standing anywhere; nor were there others cutting across the square toward the lights. The alleys were filled discreetly with neat blocks of darkness; nothing impinged on the light or the signs. They were never confused or intersected by shadow. After following the trolley tracks, the elegant tank entered a quiet wooded district. The depth of the stillness informed me that the area was quite wealthy and residential. The bottom branches of trees were denser and their leaves luxuriant. Each leaf contained within it both light and darkness; every window, every light was distant, warm, refracted, often nothing but a flash. There were no neon signs, no gas stations, and it was like running through a forest with an occasional scattering of houses. Judging by the broken light from windows half-hidden in the darkness, I surmised that all the houses in this district were surrounded by a considerable number of trees.

Seeing them and listening to the stillness, I began to think that perhaps her words about owls hooting in broad daylight were no exaggeration.

"This is quite an impressive neighborhood."

"Yes; besides mansions, there are a lot of embassies, government residences, and villas. You can take a walk tomorrow. You will see quite a number of flags and emblems."

The tank passed through the district, turned left at the end of the road, and soon came to a halt. There was a deep forest on the right, and to the left a mass of lights. As I got out of the tank, stillness and the night descended, and the area was empty of voice or sound; a complex structure of gigantic glass boxes towered up in the darkness.

We climbed up the bright stairs to the third floor and entered the room. To the front and right were huge glass walls, and as she pulled back the curtain, a dark lake seemed to open up and glisten. There was an air of deep forest beyond, but I could not see it. On the floor of the rectangular room was a carpet and on one side a single bed; on this wall there was also an all-leather convertible sofa. A soft ottoman, a round glass table, and a television set with doors were set in place, and by the glass wall a typewriter and dictionaries were neatly stacked on the desk. The bath, and kitchen opened off the wall. The tiles sparkled, the hardware shone, and there was a luxurious but subtle fragrance of toilet water. The room was solidly sumptuous but clean in every corner; all this created an air of simplicity and durability. I didn't know where to put down the soiled and worn-out knapsack, so I placed it by the door and sat down on the sofa bed to take off my shoes.

On the floor there was a large animal skin with white and brown spots, and my bare feet felt good in the long hair.

"That's a yak hide. A Tibetan cow. I bought it the other day. I worked hard for it. After buying it I found out that the long hair is nice but it sheds easily. It was stupid of me not to think of it."

She went into the bathroom and made up her face lightly, then fetched bottles of sherry, whisky, Schnapps, and ice from the refrigerator, and put them on the round table. I poured Schnapps into well-polished glasses. It was extremely cold, clouding the cut-glass pattern immediately.

"I'm amazed. Let's drink to all this."

"See, you *are* surprised."

"Astounded."

"The sofa and the bed and the desk belong to the room —the foundation furnished it. But the rest I bought piece by piece—the typewriter, the television, the yak hide—and I have more things in the basement. A lot of things. I'll show them to you tomorrow. I even have a sealskin coat. That's a conversation piece. My colleagues in the department tease me a lot; they say, 'You always dress like a Salvation Army girl, so what are you doing with that coat?' But I wanted it so badly. I wear it in the nude, and I look gorgeous. It gives me the glamour of a Mata Hari. I found that out when I took off all my clothes at midnight in front of the mirror, and made all sorts of poses."

She sat on the ottoman, slowly sipping the Schnapps, and laughed surreptitiously. Her eyes were mischievous; she was relaxed, confident, and as imposing as a ship.

"Ten years ago, when I drifted into this country," she put down the glass and spoke softly, "ten years ago, all I had was a raincoat and a suitcase, and I couldn't speak the language.

I didn't even know the ABC's. I learned, step by step, like a toddler. I felt as if I were digging up the Alps with a spoon. I don't know how many times I thought of committing suicide. I didn't want to go back to Japan even if I died. I used to cry a great deal. I washed dishes, and I sold cigarettes in cabarets. I was treated so badly that I felt pain in my very bones; I have been trampled all over. It was horrible. I'll tell you about it all some time. Since I won a scholarship, it's been relatively easy, but it was indescribable until then. I dream about it even now, and I wake up at night with a nightmare, screaming, right here in that bed. By the way, how do you like this room? Do you like it?"

"It's not a question of liking or disliking. First of all, I'm astounded. I'm still in a daze. You had told me about it, but I didn't expect it to be quite so impressive. Well, I take my hat off to you. You're great. You are magnificent. You make us men proud of you!"

"Never underestimate a woman!"

"You said it."

"I can control the temperature, and relative humidity. What would you like to have? Tell me whatever you like, and I'll make the adjustments."

"Spare me heat or air-conditioning."

"All right."

She put down the glass and went to the dial on the wall by the door, touched it briefly, and returned to her seat. The glass wall on the right was colossal, but it was made of sliding panels, and as she undid the latch, the door glided smoothly, slowly. Outside was a balcony, and a deep tide of invigorating air rising from the forest invaded the room in waves. Its biting freshness was loaded with moss, rain, shadow, and sap.

I went out to the balcony barefoot and placed the glass of Schnapps on the balustrade, after sipping a mouthful. The cold drop of liquid rolled into the darkness with a streak of heat; it exploded with a flash somewhere deep down. She came out and stood beside me, stealthily laying her cheek against my shoulder.

"How is your dissertation coming along?"

"Well, thank you. I think I can finish editing it in two or three more days. I have to send it to the binder's and present it to the faculty office, then I'll be all finished. After that, everything has to wait until this fall. Then I have to dodge, rebut, and rebuff all kinds of questions that will be coming at me from all sides. In other words, I have to defend my dissertation. But that's in the fall, and there's no way of preparing for it, because I don't know what will be asked. It's too late to fret about it; my daily work is my only weapon. So, I'm going to have a good time this summer with no regrets. Please be patient for two or three days. Then I'll cook you a pizza, chop suey, hot vegetable noodles, anything you like. If you want the hot vegetable noodles, I can even make them tomorrow. I'll go to the Asian restaurant and get the vegetables and stock from Madame Chao. It may meet your qualified approval."

"It'll be good if you put as much of yourself into it as you did into your dissertation."

"I'll cook solely and exclusively for you. A single woman's cooking can be rather subtle at times. I'm sure there's something you can sink your teeth into. They say 'eat your bread with the salt of tears'; my cooking is precisely that. It belongs in the same class as a barren womb, or a masterless dog. Would that be too spicy for you?"

"I've never tasted a soup made of women's tears, and I'd like to try it. But you're lucky. I'm envious of you because you seem to be enjoying your work; you really look as if you are happy with it."

"At my age!"

"You seemed to like to study in those days too."

"In those days, I couldn't study even when I wanted to."

She chuckled softly with a trace of bitterness in her cheerful voice. It was not a brittle sound like the shattering of glass, and I felt relieved. She seemed to be looking back over her shoulder at her misery through the shrouded past, and smiling. Her cheerfulness, too, was unfathomable to me, but at least past pain was not oozing out like poison. She had the air of a magnanimous victor. Years ago, when she laughed, she used to be sensitive and sharp, but her voice would cloud immediately; her laughter did not last long, and she always had the habit of falling into a pensive mood afterwards. Her face was angular, with high cheekbones; at times, when she was thoughtful, she looked full of life. At other times, pain was etched pathetically around her mouth. The first time I saw her was shortly after she had graduated from college. She had traveled through various countries and published a travel book. She had no steady job, but worked as a translator, a reporter. She offered to direct a Chekhov play for an amateur theatrical group made up of doctors. She enjoyed the amateur theater but she could not earn a living by it. She made the rounds of newspaper offices and magazine publishers with bits of writing, and at night she would appear, exhausted, at a restaurant or bar where I was waiting. I sometimes read her manuscripts, edited them, and gave her advice. She sat quietly and listened to me for a long time, but she often cursed or mocked the people and events she had encountered during the day, and laughed sharply. In laughter, her eyes slid aimlessly over the surface of the wall, the lamps, and liquor bottles, and in profile she looked frightened and timid most of the time. Her undaunted curiosity, indefatigable intellect, the diligence that never permitted her to be idle, and the pride that made her hide her acute bitterness behind a certain stylishness even in dire poverty—she was endowed with all these, but her eyes drifted over the edge of her glass with the bewilderment of a child at twilight. This confusion, of course, came largely from her feelings of insecurity at that time, but it took me some months to guess that she deeply dreaded a return to the indignities and wretchedness of her past. I was young and foolish, devouring the poignancy of our affair, to which her despair and unhappiness were added spice. Sweetness can only be experienced when contrasted with bitterness; but to know this requires a tremendous amount of self-sacrifice. In those days, I was never suicidal, merely rapacious about others. The reason that I knew no differently was that she, too, devoured me in rapture, responding to me with her magnificent white body. I should have known, however vaguely, that no matter what exquisite originality of technique or device was used, nor how perfect the affair, a man and a woman are ultimately dreamers of different dreams on the same bed, that they are different sexual entities, and that they are only trying each to expand his own territory and his own fulfillment. The more closely they come together and the more they expand the territories of their individual bodies, the more they fragment and become isolated. But I lacked such an acute perception. I only realized this after she let me know by letter that she had no intention of returning to Japan, thus carrying out exactly what she had jokingly hinted at several times after love-making, as we lay with our legs entwined and drank lukewarm tea. I was jolted to a recognition of my stupidity, as if I had been slapped in the face. After the shock had subsided, I contemplated all the things that she had casually but determinedly avoided talking about. After examining them, I realized anew that I had known nothing whatsoever about her. It was clearly a fantasy, mere conjecture, for me to try to find out something about her without any clues. Yet I had indulged myself in it because of something in me that felt lighter for having parted from her, and my loneliness turned into reminiscence rather than constraint. She left me only the memories of fleeting pensive moods, vague murmurs, cutting words that flashed in her jokes, vulgar words that fell from her lips in her good moods, and words of self-admonition interspersed with sudden moans in moments of breathless ecstasy. I immersed myself in these insubstantial memories on street corners, at night, feeding my imagination. Before I was aware of it, I had begun to suspect her of concealing some period of her late girlhood somewhere, scratching out a living as a concubine, or as someone's mistress, or something of the kind. It was only a wild guess; I did not have any sense of filth or unpleasantness when thinking about it. Because I wondered whether I myself could have lived through that particular period in Japan without doing something of the sort, had I been a woman and an orphan, thinking about it was poignant rather than distasteful, heroic rather than humiliating. Still, this feeling seemed to have sprung from pity—from my boyhood memory of trembling with cold and hatred in the corner of a town factory by a wintry canal. For the umpteenth time, I was trying to touch others through myself.

She whispered softly, "It seems to be getting chilly."

"Yes, so it is."

"Let's go inside."

"Yes, let's."

"Wait a minute. I'll fill the bathtub. I'll put in plenty of Badedas and make a lot of bubbles. Why don't you soak yourself in it and smoke a cigarette? You said it tastes good to smoke in the bath. And bring the Schnapps with you."

"I have athlete's foot; are you going to wash them too?"

"I'll wash you everywhere."

"You make me cry."

"Don't be funny."

She carefully picked up my glass of Schnapps and went inside, into the bright cream-colored light, to her yak hide, to her sparkling tiles and metals.

Night was approaching morning, and the room was silently waiting, full of power. As I turned the tap, hot water gushed out immediately deafening me. As she sprayed the green liquid generously over the seething water, delicate white foam rose and swelled, instantly covering the bathtub. She added two or three drops of toilet water, and the bathroom was filled with the fragrance of a spring greenhouse at ten o'clock in the morning. It was rich but not cloying, and a breath of freshness moved over the tub. The room with the window covered by the red potato sack had had an extremely temperimental hot water supply. Even when hot water did come out, the spigot constantly coughed and hiccoughed, and we could not rely on it at all. Here, everything was precision and efficiency itself, from the latch on the door to the faucet. I soaked my body in the hot water and buried myself up to the chin in foam. I was rapturously nursing a dry Schnapps in my right hand and a soft cigarette in my left, when she came in completely nude and slipped into the foam from a corner of the tub. The hot water swayed and the heat penetrated my joints to the marrow. She scrubbed my hard shinbones with her hedgehog, and washed the tender clefts between my toes with her fingers. After cleaning them thoroughly one by one, she cracked my toes firmly, making them flexible.

"Thank you."

"You're welcome."

In the warm, fragrant mist, her strong shoulders and back were moist and flushed pink. As I scrubbed her with the hedgehog and washed her down, red streaks appeared, then soon merged into the cloudy pink skin and drifted in the white foam and green water; she gleamed with inner light, the radiance of an ice palace.

"There are all kinds of bubble baths, such as ocean blue or forest moss. There's one that smells of roses. I'll buy all kinds so you can choose what you like."

"The forest moss sounds good. It's subtler than roses. I like this soap. The foam does all the washing while I just soak in it. I don't have to do anything but sit in it; it's enough to give to a lazy, bath-hater like me the incentive to take a bath."

She shows no fear, no timidity now. She stretches out to her full length in the foam, and the two of us lie together in the bathtub; she is entranced to see her radiant round shoulders emerge and submerge in the green water. I turn over and slowly penetrate her. She stops looking at her shoulders and relaxes, passively closing her eyes. She is buried up to her ears and her face alone floats in the white clouds. It brings an association to mind that she senses.

Sluggishly, she opens her eyes.

"There's a poem I wrote. I'm embarrassed to recite it all to you, so I'll give you only the first two lines. It's a lonely woman's diversion:

> The bed in the morning
> Is a coffin of marble."

She closes her eyes slowly. "How's that?"

Quietly swaying with her flesh, I reply, "You've got to tell me the rest of it."

"Some other time; soon."

I marvel at this affair, which causes me neither agitation nor fear; it neither embraces unhappiness nor provides a temporary refuge. It is simply something bright, fragrant, warm, and clean. As I move inside her against the familiar right wall,

I soon feel the habitual stirring. The point of desire comes to meet me; it stops momentarily; it pecks at me convulsively, or lightly kisses me, or dances, trembling delicately like a small insect. At times it crawls, then sometimes suddenly takes me in and squeezes. Her breasts rise and fall, flush and gleam in the foam; they appear like pink atolls bathed in the waves. I close my eyes and suddenly feel the forest penetrating the glass walls as far as the entrance of the bathroom. The meadows, the mountain stream, the sparkling golden wheat fields and twinkling lights move slowly one by one in the back of my head.

Suddenly she lifts her face. It is a vigorous movement and the bubbles scatter, the water sways, and a strong sinew stands out on her neck. She tilts her head and clears her eyes.

"I can hear it. They're here. They've come."

A smile spreads over her face.

"There they are, chirping. Chirping helplessly. Can't you hear them? There. Behind the plumbing there. Look at them. They missed me while I was away."

Remaining on top of her, I look over my shoulder and, as I concentrate my gaze on the spot to which she pointed, I see a drainage outlet behind the toilet bowl and something like two specks of shadow crawling out of the small holes in the metal cover. They begin to move timidly, hugging the wall, and disappear behind the toilet bowl. Soon, a weak chirping like a sigh or a sob is heard intermittently. Their voices are so feeble that they themselves would have disappeared without even leaving a spot on the tiles.

"They sound undernourished."

"Don't they? They exhaust themselves climbing up the pipes all the way to the third floor. By the time they really have to perform, they can hardly sing; they are hoarse. I'm worried. What can I do for them?"

"You can slice cucumbers and leave them there."

"Do crickets like cucumbers?"

"They like holes in bricks, too."

She tilted her head and listened; she smiled, and mouthed the words: cucumber, cucumber. The water was getting cooler, but warmth was pervading my body. I withdrew from her gently, washed, and stepped out of the tub.

Sweet, quiet, soft.

As I stood on the balcony and looked out, I sometimes doubted that there were any roads in the area. This happened at a certain angle of vision. Each house was surrounded by deep woods, and the lower branches often protruded over the hedge, into the road; as one looked down from the sky, everything was covered with green. The area was blanketed completely, a sea of foliage. Pointing at the trees, she told me "that's a chestnut, this is a linden tree, and that's an elm."

The residential district is hidden under this sea of foliage; a triangular red roof, a white window, or a balcony with overflowing geraniums can be seen floating here and there. As I walk down the road, I look at the houses over the hedges, hidden behind gigantic tree trunks, surrounded by lawns and flowerbeds; designed for simplicity rather than ostentation, spareness rather than luxury, they make me feel the enormity of massed wealth. Perhaps because it is the holiday season, no matter what time I walk I never hear the sound of voices or echoes from the houses. No one is seen in the street, only a few automobiles go by, and the strong first branches of linden trees throw cold shadows on the asphalt like deep pools. Birds with yellow beaks hop around the red geraniums, and sometimes squirrels are seen playing by the edge of a little culvert buried in dead leaves.

There is a forest. As I walk through it along the cool, dark lane, I come out on the bank of a large river. Somewhere far beyond, there is a rock bearing a legend of a mermaid who tempted passing boatmen. The water is muddy and yellow. Strong iron cargo boats flying the national flag of red, yellow, and black move slowly up this muddy water. On the second or third day, I heard an owl hooting in broad daylight in the forest or in the roadside trees. It was like a deep breath through a bamboo pipe, a voice trying to frighten and yet frightened of itself. There is a wayside drinking fountain at the edge of the forest, standing as if forgotten. The pipe is old and rusty, but water spurts out as I turn it on. A squirrel knows about it, but being unable to turn on the water himself, he waits patiently for someone to pass by. He stands on the brim of the basin and looks at me with his shining round eyes. He stares intently, without crying or jumping around. I come closer but he is not alarmed; he only arches his back, covered with downy gray-brown fur, and watches my hand turning the tap. As the water gushes out, he hastily drinks a tiny amount and shakes his fur at the throat, which trembles as though he were gargling, then flashes away and disappears in the forest.

I walk through the neighborhood, then an underpass, and come out on a small square. Several days a week, a market is open there. Peasants from nearby villages come, loading their trailers with produce. They sell roses and geraniums as well as vegetables and fruit. Next to the potatoes, which sweat in lumps of black mud, are roses, handled roughly by coarse fingers like gigantic slugs. But the vermillion of the flowers is so intense that the veins in the petals appear almost black; the roses are strong and proud, and never show signs of withering or dying. No matter how mistreated they are, the exquisite flowers recover their resilience and sway, never shedding a petal. As I watch, I feel a hint of something poignant, voluptuous.

Potatoes, cucumbers, onions, lettuce, broccoli, everything is there, but it seems to be the season for cherries and mushrooms. They are sold in large quantities very cheaply. She took a quantity of mesh bags out of the kitchen cupboard and went to the market, and after packing one after another with vegetables, she bought the cherries and mushrooms I had asked for, but in such quantities that she could hardly hold them in both arms; she carried them all on her back and shoulders as she walked back the long way, neither perspiring nor panting for breath. When she went to buy some soup at Professor Chao's restaurant, she took a huge thermos bottle that she borrowed from a young student, and she casually slung it over her shoulder together with the string bags and got on a bus. Most of the time, she walked; once in a while she took a bus, stingily tearing off, bit by bit, the worn-out token tickets, almost never using a taxi. If I got irritated by the chattering of women at the bus stop and by the slowness of the bus and suggested we use a taxi, she would immediately change color, protest, and start scolding me, and even after returning to her room, she still burned, muttering as she went in and out of the kitchen. According to what I could make out, it sounded as though the whole edifice built up by her ten years of toil would collapse just because she took a taxi instead of a bus with her half-used ticket. While she was so mean regarding some things, she never begrudged any extravagance when it came to eating. If she decided she wanted to eat something—lettuce, potatoes, mushrooms—she agreed to the price on the spot. She bought them in abundance and walked all the way home showing no pain, no matter how her shoulders might ache, or how unsightly she might look, or how far the journey was. If she found out that her favorite food or what she needed for a new recipe was in season and inexpensive, she would stand rapturously in front of the wagon or trailer, her mouth open like a child's. This special expression on her face would appear only when she found out that the object of her desire was cheap as well. Thrift and gluttony frequently create a dilemma, but they do not contradict each other if the food is in season and abundant. By sticking close to the seasons at all times, she seemed to have solved her problem. If I suggested buying cherries, her eyes brightened, but if I mentioned canned caviar, her eyes immediately widened sluggishly and she became apathetic. While she carried her many string bags like a Santa Claus, I followed her, watching her strong white legs move with precision, flashing their sinews under her short tartan skirt. I realized that she was devouring "the here and now," opening her mouth wide as if to guzzle down water. "Now" had pervaded her entire body, even her hair, escaping constantly from her eyelids or lips and moving vividly in her smile.

It also flowed from her hands and spread into everything, creating a cold frenzy in the glass room where the soft breeze streamed in, mingled with the hot, clear sun. She carried her mesh bags and thermos jars into the kitchen and made some quiet cooking noises for a while. Soon she brought in a large bowl of chop suey, and a large pot filled with hot vegetable noodles. The chop suey was sautéed with all kinds of vegetables and bits of meat and enough mushrooms to cover them all. She ate this food constantly, often chuckling to herself.

"I bought enough mushrooms to feed a horse, so I'll sauté them tonight. They are not bad au gratin, and I think I can use them for stew too. Then they will be wonderful marinated in oil and vinegar and served as an hors d'oeuvre. Also, I wonder how they will be in fried rice?"

"Fine. Mushrooms will be just right in fried rice. Fried rice is hard to make. People don't think much of it, but frying rice fluffily seems to take a lot of skill. Southeast Asian rice is the best for it. The Japanese don't like it because it's dry and the rice grain pops out, but they only complain because they don't know how to cook it. It's incomparable if you make fried rice or porridge with it. It has a lightness that cannot be matched by Japanese or California rice. That's the thing; Bashō advocated lightness in addition to his *wabi* and *sabi*.* The simpler the dish, the more difficult it is to cook, it seems to me."

"I think so too. Wait a minute, I'm going to make a note of it. They must have Southeast Asian rice at Professor Chao's restaurant. I'll ask them to give me some. And while I'm at it, I'll ask Madame Chao to teach me how to cook porridge. It's not a bad idea to get a recipe."

"That's an understatement. Chinese porridge is a real connoisseur's food. I don't know about the liver of a dragon or the marrows of a phoenix, but I've tried the bear's paw and swallows' nests. But a bowl of Chinese porridge beats them all. It's really good. There are all kinds, with fish, and with chicken, but I like any kinds of innards; the blood is completely washed out, so they don't smell. It has a nebulous quality. I like that. There's nothing so simple and yet with so much smooth subtlety. And you sip it squatting on the roadside behind a garbage dump, rubbing shoulders with coolies and rickshaw men. You pick up pieces of sack and tube on the end of your chopsticks; and there is a pleasure in wondering whether it is a stomach or an intestine. If you dip it in hot salad oil and eat it, it's really nice and spicy."

*Bashō, a seventeenth-century *haiku* poet; *wabi* and *sabi* are aesthetic qualities he advocated in *haiku*. [*trans.*]

"Your usual taste is showing itself."

"It's a fact that dirty eating places in the back streets very frequently tend to have good food. But whether it is in Hong Kong, Saigon, or Bangkok, those eating places in Chinatown are all totally and indiscriminately dirty; every restaurant and every vending wagon is filthy; so you don't know which one to choose. The only thing you can do is to look for the most crowded one. Phlegm, spit, snot, dog shit all over the place . . . it's quite disgusting. It takes a considerable amount of discipline to sit calmly in the midst of all the filth and brag, 'How can the power of the emperor destroy me?'* I too felt nauseated to begin with, but I was able to overcome all that with a little self-control."

"That may be true, but you like that sort of thing anyway without any effort. I doubt if you can call it self-discipline if you like it to begin with. Whether it can be called the *Aufhaben* from an obstacle, I must ask Dr. Steinkopf tomorrow when I go to school."

"I wish you'd ask me the relationship between filth and appetite. It must be because when you go to a dirty restaurant, you feel relaxed, and as you relax your stomach and taste buds are dilated, and you feel that everything is appetizing. Even steaks are better if they are rare and smell of fresh blood. It might mean that depth is achieved through impurity rather than purity. Even a novel—you write a novel with words, but words are the ultimate imprecision. They are facts and mat-

*This refers to an episode concerning Emperor Yao, a legendary wise king of ancient China, contained in the *Abridged Histories of Eighteen Dynasties (Shih pa shih lieh).* According to the story, Emperor Yao was taking a stroll one day and saw a man who was so content with his life that he boasted: "The Emperor has no power over me. I have nothing to do with the Emperor." The episode is given as an example of a perfect government, so good that people do not realize their well-being is due to the government. [*trans.*]

ters, and yet they are nothing but obscurity and there is no specific weight in their meanings. Words can take on any connotation depending on one's experience. They are constantly living and changing. You can't stop them. They collapse as soon as you pause to scrutinize them. Once in a while, you have a momentary inspiration, and you grasp that brief phrase. After you seize it, you have to turn your eyes away immediately. If you stare at it, it will instantly cloud with your fingerprints, or crumble into powder. It's like the iridescent wings of a *tamamushi* beetle. Did you ever hunt for iridescent beetles when you were a child?"

"I know about longhorn beetles."

"That's too bad."

After the meal, she makes energetic trips between the light and shadow, carrying dishes and pots into the kitchen. She is completely naked. So am I. The front glass wall is covered with curtains, and the right-hand glass doors are half covered, half open, so that the light, the heat, and the breeze will enter from the balcony. We had decided, and promised, that we would be always completely nude when we were in the room. At least, we decided to try it, and we would change it if it became too much like a habit. I wonder if, like words, human bodies are not also gossamer beneath imposed forms. I wonder if they are not continuously changing with experience, and yet remaining apparently the same. If experience means not only the dramatic but also moments of conscious laziness, her body, and mine too, must be palpitating with experiences all the time. Aside from the layers of muscle that have been especially built up for decorative purposes, human bodies in general cannot withstand visual appreciation unless they are hidden by cloth, or bound by a belt or corset, or supported. We are probably all comical seals, ugly and arrogant, fit only to provoke a burst of laughter at a glance. But

I sit down on the sofa and, feeling the cold leather against the wrinkles of my testicles, I lose myself in contemplation of the changes in her body as it moves around busily: the small shadows that flicker under her breasts and disappear; the two small dimples on her buttocks; a touch of melancholy in her gazing eyes; the delicate quivering of her pubic hair; the long, sharply defined sinews; the complex contours of her legs from thigh down to ankle; the structure and movements of many large and small bones. All these are tricks of the moment. I am afraid of her giving a domestic smell to this room and of her getting accustomed to housewifely gestures. I am trying to postpone it, even if only for a moment, or to avoid it. In my haze of uncertainty, I feel a familiar foreboding of suffocation. I wonder if she has forgotten the frog man whom she watched and laughed at, and if, unawares, she is planning to settle into the housewifely pattern.

One quiet afternoon, I was looking at the assortment of restaurant menus she had collected over the past ten years. I turned them over one by one, and looked at them, covered with illustrations of pigs, steers, fish, shells, and flowers. She was sitting quietly next to me, completely naked, and then silently stood up and thrust her legs into denim trousers. She opened the door and went down the stairs humming something. She came back from the basement bringing objects from storage. A hi-fi amplifier, a vacuum cleaner, a blender, a Danish lamp, shoes, shoes, shoes, a Persian lamb coat, a sealskin coat. She arranged these things all over the floor, like a specialty boutique in a department store, and told me that her ultrasonic washer and refrigerator were too large to move, so she had left them in the storage room. Standing in the midst of them, she pointed at the television, the yak fur, the typewriter, slowly waving her arm around the entire room, and spoke in a subdued voice:

"They are all mine. I bought them. I didn't take taxis, and I didn't even drink tea and I bought them all. How do you like it? Just look at them! Don't you think I worked hard?"

She smiled a smile that could be taken as pride or bitterness. A sense of immediacy filled her entire body and overflowed from her, sparkling and trembling at the brim. Energy and tenderness surrounded her shoulders and her elbows, which rested on her hips. She stood with her legs slightly apart and pointing at one thing after another began to tell me the laborious history of how she had accumulated these objects. Only then did I begin to see something. The astonishment that I felt about how many things a woman's loneliness could store away in ten years began to recede quietly, and a certain desolation clearly took its place. She was smiling, as though surrounded by her children or pets, but she was completely alienated. It was not because those objects had maintained the freshness with which they had come from a factory conveyor belt without any scuff marks, dirt, or fingerprints. The dishes, pans, and cups we used for the meal a while ago had some scars and spots, but even they expressed the same desolation. She was not capable of giving any imprint to the bathtub, the glass walls, the balcony, the entire room, to all the things around her body. The objects were touched, clasped, used, and produced effects, but she was only sliding cleverly over the surface of her possessions, and they turned into neither gold nor ashes under her touch, nor were they transformed into silent creatures with a life of their own. They did not play with her fingers, nor sulk, nor entwine her, nor come running to meet her. The room would be just the same whether she lived here for ten years or twenty, whether she kept it clean or dirty; when she left, it would be the same as the day she first entered it. She was living in the room but not living there at all, as it were. She was not the master of these objects but their tenant.

Therefore, that red raincoat, worn to shreds and shapeless, a crumpled thing, still did not become part of her skin, nor did it become her pet, like a dog. Even if it were folded carefully and placed on the sofa, it never waited for her, for her eyes, her voice, or her hand as a dog would.

"See, don't you think it's rather plush?"

"It looks good on you."

"I think so too."

"It was a nice thing to buy."

"I wanted someone to say that to me."

She threw off her blue jeans and was naked again, then put her sealskin coat around her shoulders and stood in front of the mirror. Winking an eye, or tilting her head, or dangling a cigarette from a corner of her lips, she paced up and down in front of me, as though crossing a theater lobby. In the light and shadow, this animal with its gleaming thick, smooth texture moved agilely, padding to the east, or hurrying to the south. But I was filled with a swelling sense of desolation, and I could barely breathe.

It was all I could do not to look away. The familiar feeling was back. It was there. The thing that I could never get used to, no matter how many times I was overpowered, was just beginning to lift its face.

Many years before, I had become acquainted with a young artist in the frog man's park. I knew nothing about him other than the fact that he was from Kyushu. He called himself an artist, but I had never seen him paint. He could talk about art and women with a penetrating insight, but about them alone, and if I let him talk about other things, he betrayed the knowledge of an elementary school child. We saw each other every day, and slumped on bar stools sipping drinks, exchanging bawdy jokes while watching the eyes and hips of the women who passed by, and indulging in sniggering laughter.

He was extremely poor, and gave off a heavy smell of dirt and oil from his worn-out green jacket; he crept out of a pitch-dark storage hut and walked along the alley walls as though having to cling to them, barely able to reach the chair where I was waiting, and all the while coaxing his stomach, which received maybe half a meal a day, or one and a half meals in two days. He was a poor talker, and looked gloomy. His eyes were sharp and dark, and sometimes he started to laugh convulsively like a child, but he was an expert in the matter of women. The faces of the girls who came to look for him at the bar were always different. They were seamstresses, shopgirls, or elementary school teachers. He offered them his penis and the women offered him sandwiches and hamburgers in exchange.

He had no money to buy paint and canvas, and the electricity had been stopped because he had not paid the rent for many months; besides, the room had no window and was pitch-black day and night. Therefore he could do nothing to pass the time but loiter in bars and let the women offer him spending money. Once I was taken to his room. It was a miserable storage room, worse than the maid's room, under the staircase, damp and filled with an unidentifiable rotten odor. He had once mentioned that he had no money to buy condoms and sometimes, when he could not help it, he withdrew and ejaculated instantaneously. So, a large part of the smell of viscous liquid protein scattered on the floor must have contributed to the odor that filled the room. Before I could feel nauseated, my eyes burned and tears leaked out. In the half light, all the junk he had picked up here and there was piled on the floor, walls, all over the place: a toilet seat cover, a bicycle wheel, a doorknob, a piece of gas pipe, a water spigot, a horseshoe, all kinds of automobile parts, a broken monkey wrench, a jack, a hammer, and so forth. He showed me a flat iron pan like a fan, for baking Italian cookies, saying that he had just found it two days before. It probably was discarded in a garbage dump somewhere behind the railroad station.

"This is fine, this thing. Don't you think so? It's nifty. We can't imitate this sort of thing. I'm falling in love with it. I wonder which is better, a lay or this thing!"

In the darkness, he lowered his voice and narrowed his eyes, repeatedly caressing the broken iron pan. Up and down, right and left, slowly, or rapidly, he rubbed the object with his hand, which was mere skin and bone. He seemed to be moved from the depths of his heart, and I suspected that he was on the verge of ejaculation. He caressed the old iron with an almost obscene amount of tenacious attachment, with the fondness of a blind man's hand; he had quite forgotten that I was beside him. While I was watching the hand and the old iron, I had a shock. The old, rusted, brittle red disk suddenly crept out of shape, and in the midst of filth and corrosion, the iron softened, became tender, and began to frisk playfully with a coquettish purr, twisting its body. It is said that a certain king was able to transform everything he touched into gold, but this artist was changing it into a living thing. I could not do that. I have tried many times; but I only succeed in leaving fingerprints on things. I can neither see objects nor grasp their essence. Several days later, I took off my trousers, presented them to him, and left for the airport, but this memory stayed with me for a long time.

Does she recognize her alienation? Does she feel that she is in some way deformed? The solitude I sense vaguely in her is like an echo of her past. She is intoxicated with the here and now, moves vivaciously, acts with confidence, and lets objects serve her; she doesn't pay any attention to her desolation and pathos. I will not point this out to her. Even if I let her know, it will only permit her to sense my own weakness, while she

(71)

will come out of it unscathed. Even if she is still a captive of her past, since I don't really know anything about it, her misery is nothing more than something transparent that flickers and in an instant disappears, and I will probably feel that the whole thing has been an optical illusion. It may be something that will simply pass away. I realized all this one day, at noon. My whole body was flushed with a Schnapps hangover, and I lazed on the sofa, my forehead and chest bathed in the bright sunlight. I dozed, unable to decide whether I should get up or not. The breeze from the forest circled once around the balcony and streamed into the room; muffled cries of a turtledove echoed somewhere. Suddenly, there was the sound of the key turning, the door opened, and she dashed in.

Standing at one side of the sofa, she stared at me with a peculiar look in her eyes. Probably having run up the stairs, she was a little out of breath, and her breasts were heaving. Her calmness hid the urgency of a flying arrow.

"Finished! I've finished it! The dissertation is all bound. I just got it from the bookbinder. Here, look, it's magnificently heavy. I'm going out again in the afternoon to hand it over to Professor Steinkopf. Then I'm all done, everything's finished. The die has been cast and I don't know what the result is going to be, odds or evens."

She took a thick book out of the mesh bag and placed it quietly on my chest, and, pacing up and down the room, chanted in a small voice:

"Don't know, don't know, I don't know!"

The book was bound in a thick, hard, dark-green cover, and a good-quality, ivory-colored paper was inserted between the cover and the text. The body of the book was printed in a neat, small typeface. I could not read one word of it, but I knew that ten years' work was condensed into it. Her solitude, fear, and diligence were crystallized in the volume. I turned the pages, smelled the ink, and caressed the book. If I felt desolation in her sealskin coat, I should have felt something in the book too. But could I have been mistaken in that moment? Could that desolation have been a shadow projected by me and not something that originated from her? Or could it be that the exaltation that radiated from her all over now happened to overshadow her misery for the time being?

"Splendid! It's admirable!"

She turned around and laughed. "Don't say that lying down!" she scolded me. "Get up and say it."

I rose from the sofa, and shook hands with her. Her palm was firm, with meticulously constructed bones; yet it had something fragile about it.

Later in the afternoon, after she returned from the university, we waited together for evening to come, and then went to town to drink wine. We walked through the residential area, traversed the forest, crossed the river by ferry, and after walking along the opposite bank for a while, we arrived at the wine tavern just as we began to perspire. She told me that the place went back three hundred years, and served bottles without a label, but its fame had spread far and wide like dandelion seeds. We walked through an old gateway of strong square timbers, and came to a red brick courtyard; large barrels, horse carts, and grape baskets were scattered around, and a huge, overripe tomato of a woman appeared, smiling.

"Dry or sweet, which would you like?"

"We should first try a little bit of each. After that we'll decide which we like, and then we will drink to the finish. Let me worry about the payment. It's a celebration for you. I don't want to talk about anything but food and the glow of the evening sun. And when we go home, we'll take a taxi. Spare me the rumbling bus."

"All right. I agree. And the wine—there are all kinds, Auslese, Spätlese; which shall it be?"

"Leave it to that Tante, and ask her what will be the best for tonight. Let's do that. We can't go wrong."

"OK!"

Listening to her explanation, the gigantic tomato woman laughed, almost burst open in a splash of juice; then she muttered a few words and disappeared into the main quarters.

The wine was soon brought over to the oak table, which was so thick and strong that if I had carelessly dropped my elbow on it, I might have been hurt. Both glasses, the dry and the sweet, were clouded with cold condensation, but when the evening sun touched it, the glass of dry wine turned into a light gold, the one with sweet wine turned into a gold of a darker hue, and the glasses looked as though a miniature arctic sun were contained in each. The dry wine slipped down my throat like water, and the sweet wine left a hint of aroma in the mouth. After the second glass, we settled on the dry wine and drank that alone until nine o'clock.

She bent her head and wept a little.

Once again, I began to feel sleepy.

After formally submitting the dissertation, she said she had some unfinished duties remaining from before the vacation and went out once a day, combining the trip with shopping. I accompanied her two or three times. It was a very short bus ride to the city from where we lived. It might be a capital, but it was just as small in the daylight as it was when I looked at it by streetlight at night. There were some large department stores, but old trolleys crept past the railroad station, and the sound of their bells was not even drowned out by the noise of taxis; you could hear each quite clearly. I am not good at memorizing geography, but soon a general map of the capital, the size of the palm of my hand, became part of me. I strolled around the university campus, peeped into markets, and asked to see the spoon hooks for trout fishing and the collection of artificial flies at a fishing tackle shop. I drank tea under the chestnut trees and ate simple meals in the glass-walled restaurant on top of a hill at the edge of town.

Up to now, the sun had been weak, but it finally began to take on intensity and heat, especially in the afternoon. Inertia lay over everything in the dazzling brilliance. The light began to loosen and blur. All the shop windows were polished until they were as dark as deep pools; behind them was the flash of oily cheeks and slow-moving shadows. I became fond of certain parts of the dark lane leading up through the forest to the hill, the thriving market place, and old back alleys, but after I had familiarized myself with the rough geography, I stopped going out. No matter how she urged me, I made all kinds of excuses not to move from the couch. She seemed to be thinking of giving a pizza party, inviting Professor Steinkopf, a poet-reporter, her colleagues, and students, in order to introduce me to them, but I kept giving her unenthusiastic, vague answers.

I pull a table to the side of the couch and place a bottle of Schnapps and a glass on it. Next to these, a pile of newspapers, weekly magazines, and books, which she buys every time she goes out. She carefully selects them at station counters and bookstores from material in languages I can read, but I don't have the strength to read through one article. After two or three lines, sleep is already close around the corner, though I have just awakened from a nap. The Schnapps I drank before

I went to sleep is mixed with nicotine and my mouth is heavy and tastes foul. I wash it all down with a new glass of Schnapps, close my eyes, and sink down slowly. I can sleep any length of time. If I make up my mind to sleep, I can. The leather on the couch is beginning to take on an indistinct but definite dent in its outline and its creases hold the shape of my supine body. By turning over once or twice, I can find the hollow easily; I don't even have to do that; just by lying down, my body can roll into the dent. The night I first came to the room and glanced at it, the couch was like a thoroughbred, but it has transformed itself into an obedient and everyday beast.

I can't read, or feel, or think. Thick, viscous sleep spreads through my body, and I sink down the way a large, square crate sinks into mud. As a multitude of soft tendrils creeps up soundlessly to sway in my brain, my abdomen, or anywhere else that I feel, I begin to doze off . A breeze from the balcony caresses the soles of my feet. Each wrinkle of my limp, damp scrotum is stroked by a gentle, feathery wind. I feel myself floating away. I fall asleep from the soles of my feet to my balls; I begin to lose shape and weight from there on up. Slowly, I pull a blanket over my bare belly, drifting in an immense vacuum that is too large to touch, sometimes clear and sometimes hazy. Somewhere in the numbness of my brain I feel a desire to go somewhere devoid of books and discussions, but at the same time, I feel that there is no such thing as no-man's-land. Then, after a while, I feel that this is it; it's an uninhabited island surrounded by glasses, an island in the sky.

There is no voice, no sound. Sometimes the telephone rings, and if she is in the room, a fountain of high-pitched talk and laughter spurts for a while, but that is all. According to her, the building is occupied by scholars from Chile, Japan, India, and Scandinavia, but no one comes to visit. I don't even leave the room, so I never encounter these scholars on the staircase. She often suggests that we hold a pizza party, but each time I am frightened by the idea and make her give it up, almost in entreaty. Meeting strangers, shaking hands, arguing, watching for the changes of expression in their eyes, and in doing so, searching for other men's eyes and profiles over the shoulders of the one I am talking to, the crossfire of words that suddenly fly from left and right, front and back, like a Ping-Pong ball . . . as I think about such vacuous irritation, think about shaking their clammy, gigantic, perspiring, tool-like hands I want to back away. The mere effort of not falling off the couch is all I can manage now. I am not in a position to socialize with people. Even if I put on my shoes and go outside, the only thing I can do is turn on the water tap for the squirrel, or hold on tight to an edge of the table so that I do not slip off the chair.

"No one says anything, but I know. I know perfectly well. Here and in the department at school, they are all whispering to each other and grinning. They are all talking about how I went away for a weekend and came back with a man I picked up somewhere. 'She turned out to be a woman after all,' or 'Nature is stronger than will power,' and so forth. Some of them must be saying, 'It's good for her to have caught a man, but he does nothing but sleep and he's shadowless, a sandman. A lonely woman must feel it's better than not having any man at all even if she's unhappy.' I know all about them. But I don't care. I don't care at all. Please sleep as much as you like."

Coming back from outside, she starts talking fast, with a smile that could mean sarcasm or injured pride, and she takes off her bra and bikini underpants. She is transformed into a voluptuous nude and hangs an apron from her neck. It is an apron with appliqués of Popeye, Mickey Mouse, and Donald Duck, a kindergarten-teacher type of apron. She hides her entire front with it, but as she walks into the kitchen, I can see her back with the red ribbons flying around her neck, and her shoulders, spine, and buttocks all exposed. Mountains of white flesh tense and relax, left and right.

Sometimes I feel as though I were floating somewhere in the sky. Because the night is so quiet and clear as I hover between waking and sleeping, the large glass box feels as though it too were floating somewhere in the sky; the glass wall and the sofa fade away, and I am drifting up there, all naked. This sensation runs clearly through my whole body. I lie on the couch on this side, and she uses the bed by the opposite wall and either reads a book or sleeps. It is the time when only the soft cream-colored light of the lamp and a faint aroma of fennel from the Schnapps are present in the room. The wind does not leave footprints at such hours, and the owls do not hoot; only the deep presence of night and the forest can be felt, and my disjointed but constant recollections seem to be of nothing but distant, quiet scenes. I slip out of the confines of my flesh and evaporate, leaving used fat and consciousness behind me. Then I achieve solitude without loneliness, freedom without irritation. Ever since my childhood, I have often been tormented by the recurring dream of a sudden fall in the dark, in addition to dreams of taking entrance examinations or being chased by a bull. In the far distance below, there is a small, shining particle, and I know it is the earth. I plunge straight toward the sparkling dot no larger than a sesame seed, but somewhere in my body I feel that a spacious, vast prairie with deep, luxuriant grass is down there. Yet, I don't know whether I can ever reach it safely. Without any thought of the possibility that I may crash and be shattered into pieces, only the idea of not reaching it frightens me. I fall with a nervous insecurity that freezes me completely, and I begin to twist, almost urinate compulsively, and then wake up.

I find myself with open eyes; my hands and feet under the coverlet are numb, rigid, and cold. Ever since I first had this dream, no matter how old I was, I always remembered it as soon as I glanced at an area of darkness without tangible boundaries. However, its conditions seem to be changing now. The dream does not recur when I see the darkness of the leather. I drift only in the night sky, as relaxed as a jellyfish and evaporating, escaping from my forehead and shoulders.

In the morning, my shape is restored to me. The freedom of abandonment is gone. I am imprisoned in a large, fat bag, my face covered with clammy grease and perspiration, and I am lying on the couch or on the yak fur. Consciousness touches me with the sunlight; it is all right while I am dozing, but soon, pursued by a certain mercilessness, I start to float to the surface. The room is barred by light and shadow like a steep canyon, and summer's progress is daily tangible in the brilliance of the sun, the breeze, and the heat. I seem to be lying inside some gigantic, brilliant fruit, filled with sparkling juice, and judging by the fact that the strength is slowly but surely dwindling from my legs, I feel as if I am turning into an earthworm that does nothing but eat and defecate. I rise slowly and go into the bathroom. I soak in water hot enough to burn, the Schnapps is squeezed out together with a bitter gall, and when I have a too much residue in me, the hot water sometimes smells of alcohol. After immersing myself in hot foam with the fragrance of forest moss, and sitting immobile for quite a while, I suddenly rise and take a cold shower. The formless mass turns into a body, and the budding leaves and vines of the flaccid organism disappear. I wash my face with cold water, rinse my mouth, and gargle. I massage my face, twisting, pinching, gathering, and kneading it; it seems to work while I do it in cold water, but after I finish and peep into the mirror, the face of a middle-aged man, oily, sallow, and shapeless, appears in the glass. Filth has oozed out in blotches here and there and there is nothing to be done. I want to turn my face away as soon as I see it.

I go into the kitchen and find a plate covered with a napkin on the stainless steel worktable. I remove the napkin, to reveal a sandwich and a piece of paper. I eat the sandwich standing up, and take a small bottle of beer from the refrigerator. Wherever I look, at pots, frying pans, dishes, bowls, jars —everything is polished, shiny, and as neatly put away as ever, and not a spot of dirt or grease to be found; the whole kitchen looks like a model room in a kitchen equipment company. Sometimes I have watched the movements of her buttocks as she worked there, and I have been moved to come up behind her and embrace her, but now I can feel no hint of such an impulse.

The note says: "Thought for the day: sleeping equals fat."

Yesterday it was different. It read: "Thought for the day: falling asleep easily is a sign of youth."

I finish eating the sandwich and drinking the beer and feel a little more purposeful. I feel: now I am going to put on a pair of trousers, cover myself with a shirt, brace my belly by tightening a belt, protect my feet with a pair of shoes, and assume a shape that disguises my actual body; then I will run down the staircase into the summer day outside. But this ambition evaporates without trace before I have taken three steps, and with a faint sensation of beer stirring in my intestines, I walk back to the couch. As soon as I see the wrinkles on it with the shape of my supine form, I fall into it irresistibly and slowly close my eyes. The wrinkles absorb me without a sound, and close around me tenderly. Immediately various parts of my body begin to feel detached and my shape starts to dissolve. I sink in, swaying slowly.

In the afternoon, she rushes back. Sometimes I am startled by the sudden turning of the key. As soon as she comes in she takes her clothes off, hangs an apron around her neck, and paces up and down, telling me what she has heard and seen on campus or in town, with accompanying gestures and mimicry. She pulls up the ottoman and settles on it, placing between her legs a big can filled with "persimmon seeds" sent by her friend in Japan; she starts to munch the crackers, chattering away endlessly. I don't go out to socialize with people, but the students' gossip filters down to me through her, and I half listen to it, dozing off. And as I am listening, my eyes drift, in spite of her words, and trace the way in which her breasts, navel, pubic hair, and the labia majora appear and disappear behind the apron when she gets up or sits down. Sometimes I get up and push her down and suck her, sometimes wet and sometimes dry, and then return to the couch to urge her to continue her talk. She sits up, straightening her disheveled hair, her eyes a little distant, and settles herself again on the ottoman, continuing the gossip about Professor Steinkopf. Having been hounded both by radical students and by domestic problems, he has begun to drink day and night.

After chatting for a while, she invariably says: "What did you do today? Tell me."

There is no other way of answering, so I simply reply, "I slept."

She smiles wryly and mutters: "You said that yesterday, too."

"And I said it the day before yesterday, too," I add.

"Are you always like this when you go abroad?"

"I'm the same way even in Tokyo."

"Whenever I see you, you are sleeping. I am impressed, rather than disgusted. I sometimes think it may be a sort of genuine talent. You must be really mentally worn out. You are, I'm sure. So you act as though you have sleeping sickness. Sometimes I worry that you may be dead."

"I am as good as dead."

"For a corpse you snore rather magnificently. I feel relieved when I hear you, knowing that you are alive. When I'm shopping in the market, I sometimes have a strange feeling that I may be a woman hiding a gangster or keeping a pimp. It's not bad, but you don't even take a step out of the apartment; you stay absolutely horizontal. I'm glad that you are not a lot of bother, but you are a little bit undependable. I'm in that sort of mood these days."

"I'm worn out."

"So it seems."

"I really am wearing out."

"You don't go out, you don't like parties, you don't like gossiping, you don't want to see anyone. Right? You don't read newspapers, don't read a single book, don't watch television, don't listen to the radio. It's all 'Don'ts.' Occasionally, you seem to go out in the evening, and I think, my goodness he's really going out; then I find out that you are only going to give water to the squirrel. A minute later you're back, and you go to bed again. You just got up a minute ago, and you go back to sleep the next. You fall asleep between the time I go into the kitchen and the time I come out. There's something childlike about you. I knew some children who used to dash out of the house and not come back for half a day or a whole day, and as soon as they returned they would roll into bed and fall asleep."

"That's right. I'm like that."

"You mean you are a child?"

"Men are children no matter how old they are."

"That's what's difficult for women to understand," she

said. "That is why trouble always starts. We don't understand you at all. Men may all look the same, but there are some things that put us on guard every time. Mostly it's the child in a man. We owe most of the troubles and stupendous achievements in the world to that. They don't listen when they are told: 'Be still, Tarō,' and before you know it, Tarō is scheming to build a tower that reaches the sky and trying to bring his scheme off. The trouble starts there. If, for a change, he's quiet, he's a Rip Van Winkle; he sleeps for years. We feel like screaming: 'What is this all about?' "

"It's nature's mischief as you always say."

"You don't say it's God's?"

"It's nature's."

"Is it really a force beyond will power?"

She props her elbows on her lap, picks the rice crackers from the oil can between her legs, and begins to nibble them; after a moment of silence in which she looks serious, she sighs and stands up.

But her pizza is excellent. I must admit that. I don't get up any more unless it's to screw, eat, or shit, but I enjoy the pizza she bakes for me. She mixes yeast in the batter and kneads and kneads, and lets it rise for hours; she waits until the cells ferment in every particle and the dough gets tender and fragrant. Then she rolls it and pats it until it is as flat and round as a fan, and she piles it with plenty of mushrooms, salami, anchovies, ham, bacon, tomatoes, and pimentos, and she doesn't forget the green capers pickled in salt and vinegar either; she decorates the edge with olives and sprinkles the whole thing with an abundance of cheese and tomato sauce. When she takes it from the oven, she puts it on a large plate that she borrowed somewhere, and rushes out of the kitchen, holding it at eye level. In the delicious, hot, fragrant, buttery steam, the yellow of the melted cheese and the red of the

(83

tomato sauce glow like neon lights. I slice a piece and take a big bite into the soft ripe part near the center; all at once, sour, bitter, sweet, peppery, and salty tastes begin to explode joyfully in my mouth. It's a rustic pancake, but the ingredients have plenty of leavening: the strength of flavor withstands its yeasty richness. For this, I can't help but rise from the couch.

"You neatly avoided me with your story of porridge when I made the hot pressed vegetable noodles, but I'm sure of this. I think I can pin you down with it. I've tested it tens of times already. This is the work of a professional who pretends to be an amateur. This is the ideal food, or something close to it. You'd better believe it."

"Great. Splendid. Perfect."

"Don't talk about Chinese porridge."

"I won't."

"It's sweet of you to talk about other dishes instead of criticizing my cooking, but for a chef, it struck home. Though it taught me a good lesson."

"This is delicious. It's truly excellent. It's like being in Italy. It is strong, has body, and pulses with flavor. Nutrition and indulgence are dancing hand in hand. It really tastes like that. I'm going to get sleepy again."

"That's all right. Go ahead and sleep. They say, the way to one's heart is through one's stomach; but if I follow the way to your stomach, you'll be asleep by the time I reach your heart."

"It's a rare dish that can put a man to sleep comfortably."

"Thank you."

"Besides, let me say a word on this: a truly good sleep is achieved only once or twice out of three hundred and sixty-five days in a year, and even that cannot be guaranteed. A real masterpiece of a sleep is extremely hard to come by. At present, that's what I am thinking about. Just because one is asleep doesn't mean that one is enjoying it. Most sleep is mediocre, stupid, wasteful, I want you to know that. It's not easy."

The cheap red wine, in a bottle wrapped in straw up to its neck, stung and scraped my tongue, but the mellow depth of the pizza made me forget it.

She ate and drank, talking copiously about the past and the difficult history of pizza-making and its reputation in the department, and soon began to discuss her wish to bake it again in a week's time in order to invite Professor Steinkopf to dinner. The Professor is separated from his wife and wants to marry his secretary, but because he is Catholic and his divorce will not be recognized, he doesn't even want to go on a vacation. He has sealed himself up in the research office at the University or in his study at home. There is a rumor that one night last week his wife put a chair in front of his office door and kept vigil all night. She neither shouted nor knocked; she just sat in the chair and wept quietly all night, but the Professor kept the door closed. His colleagues have all sorts of interpretations, but from the female viewpoint, this is a tragedy of personalities. One cannot solely and exclusively blame the Professor, his wife, or the secretary; by the same token, one cannot sympathize with any one of them.

"I can invite the Professor, with the excuse to introduce you two; I want to console him. It's been too terrible for him. You won't have to talk about anything specific or difficult. You can just make small talk, about fishing, for instance. He is a very heavy drinker, so you two will get along famously. That's right, talk about alcohol. I think he'll be very pleased."

"I want to sleep."

"I know you are tired, and you are sick. It's better to believe that. But, once in a while, don't you think you might meet someone, just once? Don't you think it would do you good? You can sleep again after the party. As a matter of fact you'll be able to sleep very well after such excitement. I know you don't like parties, but there will be only one guest, the Professor. You must let me keep face sometimes."

"I'm wearing out. I'm almost worn out now. I feel suffocated just thinking about meeting a stranger, greeting him and shaking hands. I feel crushed by a mountain avalanche. I try not to think about what to do in the future by postponing it from day to day. Can't you possibly leave me alone? I beg you."

"You don't think about me at all, do you?"

"That has nothing to do with it."

"You only love yourself. You may not even do that."

The warmth and gaiety spread by the pizza vanished. A cold, sharp edge appeared in her eyes and in her voice. It was a clear indication of what I had somehow been avoiding. She glanced at my face and then away; suddenly she rose quickly, nimbly and began to carry the plates, forks, and wine bottle into the kitchen.

A nameless depression begins to spread like liquid filth. It oozes out of me, forms a pool, and creeps up my legs, soaking me up to the hip. The incomprehensible bewilderment and discomfort I feel every time I hear the word "love" stirs slowly, hidden in the gloom. Every time I hear the word, I feel something poignant and vague, something at once obscure, dim, and shapeless and I fall into a trance. It is as if I were looking out into another world, from a transparent, flexible, but impenetrable shell-like membrane. I can see a number of women's faces, eyes, bare shoulders in the dim distance. Every woman mouths almost the identical words that showered upon me just now. One woman waits until the echoes of love-making fade away, and then calmly raises her face and tells me that I am incapable of loving even myself. Another comes to a restaurant one early afternoon for the sole purpose of telling me the same thing, and states that I fell in love with the lower half of the female body but couldn't care less about the upper half, and furthermore, that I didn't even know how to make the effort to get interested in it. She eats a full-course meal and leaves the restaurant. Another woman also, after the resonance of caresses begins to fade, suddenly lifts her face from between my thighs while performing a meticulous but apathetic fellatio and says that I am merely conjuring words out of thin air.

Every time, it gives me a sudden and deep-cutting jolt. The precision of the words hits me right where it can wound me. When I am nowhere near talking about the subject, these women suddenly snatch words out of the air and utter them, and while I am trembling with astonishment, they act as though they had already forgotten about them and start to talk vivaciously about something infinitely removed from the perception that flared in them a moment ago, about the ice cream at such and such store having had flour added to it. Then, if my attention wanders off, the interrupted theme suddenly makes a new appearance, and a second thrust of aphorism comes out of their mouths to threaten me. There seems to be some continuity, and yet perhaps not; the words pierce me as nothing else can and yet their stupidity is unsurpassed. What is traumatic is the penetrating shrewdness of these women who speak such unexpected words at the most unexpected moments. As soon as they fall from their lips, the words take on a quality and weight of their own and forge ahead. The women disappear the minute they speak the words, but the one who suffers from the sharpness of the splinter seems to be only me. I wait to see how far the words will lacerate my membrane and flow into me. But the more women try to distill "love" the more frightened and unsure I become. All words contain many opposing meanings, vague and full of possibilities, but the vocabulary required to point up the subtlest nuances of human affairs seems both microscope and telescope, and I become uncertain of where to place myself in this cosmos. If I am asked by a woman whether I "like" her white buttocks, I can answer clearly in the affirmative. But if I am asked if I "love" them, I cringe before answering. If it is not a woman's behind, but a "heart" or "me," I cringe even more. Men feel attachment to the concrete and aim at the abstract, but women attach themselves to the abstract and yet try to indulge themselves with the concrete. All my nerves concentrate on the tip of my penis and the ring around the glans, and while drenched in perspiration, I still think about other things. But a woman is conscious only of her vagina with an enviable self-oblivion that galvanizes her entire body. "Love" is floating in the air far beyond. Yet, in spite of this, as soon as the play is over, "love" is suddenly called back in front of the curtain, as though nothing else could be the star.

Sinewy white thighs and calves are walking to and fro in my line of vision, her long sharp muscles flexing sharply. I am about to doze off, filled with pizza and red wine, but my sleepiness is disturbed by the aura of irritation. She is imposing, isolated, and seems to be angry. After washing the plates, she comes out of the kitchen and sits on the ottoman, a little way away from me, and turning her face to the glass wall, begins to nibble on the crackers with dignity. Behind her apron, the magnificent white breasts are moving gently.

"Sitting there like that, you look like Kintaro, the strong boy. That thing you're wearing is just like Kintaro's cinch. Instead of his mark, you have a Popeye on it. It's an amusing sight."

Usually she tops me with her quick, sharp humor. After saying it, I shut my mouth in a hurry, but it is too late. She suddenly throws the crackers into the can, stands up, discards the apron, which leaves her quite naked, quickly puts on her bra and blue jeans, and even her shirt.

She crinkles her nose and mouth to spite me, runs over to the bed and jumps in. She turns to the wall and doesn't say another word. A thought flashes through my mind that she might get angry, but I have opened my mouth, I cannot stop; I have to say what is on my mind. She gets angry after all.

I can no longer distinguish one day from the next. She stopped mentioning parties long ago. She told me in detail about the Professor's appearance and his personal affairs, since she was his female disciple who knew everything, but she never spoke again of wanting to give a pizza party to console him. Often, in her stray glances or in some casual conversation, I felt that she still wanted to talk about it but was holding back with an effort; but such impressions drifted past and vanished. After she finished the remaining duties in the seminar room, she was no longer required to go to the campus, and she stayed at home, cooking and reading books, going out only to shop for food and newspapers. Sleeping, eating, chatting, reading, then sleeping again. That is all, day after day. Occasionally, in the evening, when the daytime heat subsides, we go out for a stroll, but we select a road where we have little chance of meeting anyone, and after giving water to the squirrel, we go through the forest, look at the river for a while, and return.

One evening, which was not particularly outstanding in any way, we happened to be on the balcony when we heard the clinking of glasses. We were leaning against the cheap deck chairs she had purchased at a summer sale bargain counter, and she was drinking iced tea while I was sipping Schnapps. The gentle dewy freshness that always appeared at dusk was hovering in the air, and the sky and the forest quenched the heat that had lasted all day, finally melting into one another. Just then, the sound of clinking glasses and men's and women's laughter came from somewhere. Only the faintly glowing evening sky and the sea of foliage were visible from the balcony; it was as if, in passing through the woods, we had chanced upon the merry, scintillating laughter of a group of men and women gathered in the forest. The voices were soft and pleasant, but a crystalline echo remained a while in the clear, limpid evening, and then faded away. I was forced to realize that for a long time we had been living without seeing anyone, without talking, or drinking with other people. I felt as though I had received some sort of signal.

She tilted her head. "They are having a party," she murmured. "I wonder if it's the Indian Embassy."

I sipped the cold Schnapps in silence. A vivid envy stirred in her voice; it sounded as though it might take flight at any moment. I distinctly sensed a renewed energy that rose in her in the cool of the transparent evening and bubbled over like fresh milk foaming in a pail. She was irritated; summer had trapped her in the glass box and in her womb, and she wanted to get out of her skin. She wanted to sail like a ship, laughing and joking, into the sparkling light, to people, fragrance, and words.

"It may not be the Indians. I think they were more to the west. I think that's some African embassy. Liberia, Gabon, Zambia, and other small countries are bunched together in that area. I can't judge by the flags, and besides, they all have small, round, hard heads like the tips of matches. I really can't tell them apart."

She laughed softly, amicably. The overt envy had disappeared from her laughter, to be replaced by the endurance of a nurse who is determined not to move from the side of a patient though she dreamily looks out of the window. I felt pity for her, feeling that patience and energy were quietly but fiercely struggling beneath her air of resignation. I had stretched out in the dusk, which was filled with the cool, faint odor of moss; I sank like a lead weight, silently sipping the Schnapps. Her unhappiness was returning because of my eccentricity, but I couldn't do anything about it. All I could do was pour Schnapps into my glass.

I can no longer tell the day before yesterday from yesterday or today. Lying on the couch, I play with the same sort of fragmented recollections every day. Yet, these days, I prefer to be half dozing, half awakening, floating on the surface of sleep, rather than actually sleeping. I do all I can to avoid opening my eyes and to stay in a drowsy mood; this only serves to blot out the divisions between the days. The leather of the couch has sagged limply under my belly, back, and head. I once had thought of it as a thoroughbred leather steed, swiftness itself, which had gradually turned into an obedient practice horse; but by now it has turned into a packhorse with ragged bones and flabby, loose muscles and legs. One packhorse is lying and sleeping on top of the other every day. The days slide in and out of the same scabbard, and from my horizontal position I watch yesterday insert itself, fit in snugly up to the hilt, and withdraw uneventfully.

In my dreams, I no longer fail an entrance examination, or am chased by a bull, or drop precipitously to earth; but, instead, of late I have begun to write sentences. I invariably write these sentences just before waking. They seem like a passage of a novel or an essay, and the theme develops easily, prolifically, right under my watchful eyes; many secondary themes expand with beautiful branches, the entire structure creating a refreshing, deep, and delightful shade. While the main theme continues to develop clearly, subplots cleverly appear here and there; the plot lines are stated magnificently, and the subliminal motivations also emerge lucidly but subtly, and individual words shine one by one, glistening like lush leaves washed by rain, growing into a rich foliage that covers the plots, improvisations, and the combinations of chance and necessity. The theme always appears in the form of a single tree, and while I am absorbed in tending it, I am watching it with a third eye from a little farther away, and I am infatuated more by its clarity of outline than anything else; I lose myself in admiration of the superbly skilled development. But when I wake, and my tarnished consciousness returns in the bare light of day, this splendid structure vanishes without a trace, and I cannot even remember whether it was a novel or an essay. Only the echo of my awareness of the magnificent lucidity remains like a curl of smoke as fine as a thread, and I only know that it was definitely more than just a dream.

Still dozing, I try to evaluate the dream that is now turning its back and leaving me; I wonder whether I should call it mediocre or a poor excuse of a dream. I pry and search to see if I do not sense remains of fatigue and numbness; whether I am not marred by perspiration and body odor or am thoroughly agitated. I decide that it is as difficult to imagine an ideal sleep as it is to imagine an ideal wine. I think drowsily: appetite, sexual desire, sport, work, thought, mental torment, pleasure, everything, life itself should take place solely in sleep, and yet, only matters and events that take place before and after sleep are discussed and evaluated; is it not an injustice and terrible neglect on our part? Why is it that it is only the aftertaste of a dream that is discussed, if at all, and why is it that many writers do not devote themselves to describing sleep as much as they do sex? Drifting on dim, vague, and hazy waves, I try to think about the objects on which I have slept for the past forty years: quilts, beds, foam rubber, down, straw, hammocks, chairs, benches at railroad stations, train coaches, meadows, floors of freight cars, baled cargoes, pavements, ridges between rice fields, village roads, behind garbage dumps, on dead leaves in a jungle, on the bellies of women—it has been almost enough to make me dizzy. In spite of the fact I came into intimate contact with almost too many places and too great a variety of objects, I have forgotten most of these things, and those I can remember are pitifully few. Should this not be called ingratitude? How is it that my obliviousness runs so deep?

The opium sleep retains a definite form in my memory among countless others that have vanished. There is nothing dramatic about it, and yet it stands in isolation like a rock in the ocean, showing its face to me. I can remember almost nothing of the feelings I experienced immediately after smoking opium, except for the sluggish looseness of the entire body and joints, although I experienced it twice. Yet, I remember distinctly the sleep that I tasted as a second wave of sleep, which came to me in bed, after I had returned to the hotel. The freshness was completely unexpected and the feeling of surprise might have helped the memory. Even after an excessive drinking bout and suffering from a terrible hangover the next morning, if I have a series of customary rituals such as taking an Alka Seltzer, sipping hot tea with a pickled plum in it, and immersing myself in a hot bath, if I sleep once more, the second sleep is sometimes unexpectedly refreshing. With both of my experiences with opium, the second session of sleep was excellent.

It was after a violent terrorist action in the junior high school behind the Don Kan bar in the Cholon district of Saigon. It was an ordinary, shabby school. The report was that four teachers, men and women, were eating lunch in a class-room, and a middle-aged woman guarded by two young men suddenly appeared and fired a Mauser revolver at random, then left the room. I reached the site twenty or thirty minutes later. One of the teachers had died instantly, and three were critically wounded, I heard, but the bodies had already been removed and a pool of blood lay on the tile floor. Human beings bleed copiously when shot in the head. The blood was already beginning to coagulate, and it was piled up like lumps of raw flesh or intestines rather than clots of blood. Sandals, glasses, tea cups, chopsticks were scattered around, and an oily, almost obscene, odor was wafted through the room. The rice bowls were filled with rice, and the large bowl had some soup in it. The rice was swimming in blood, and the soup looked as though ketchup had been dissolved in it.

The cause of the incident was unknown. I asked at the police station, asked newspaper reporters, and inquired at the information agency of the Vietnamese government, but no one knew. Such things occurred daily in Saigon, and no one seemed to be particularly interested in the incident. If one pressed the point, it was rather unusual that the terrorist was a middle-aged woman, but that criterion applied only to other countries; in Vietnam, a female noodle vendor or an eighteen-year-old typist could turn into a terrorist overnight. Whether it was a struggle between Chinese immigrants and the Viet-namese, or a private lynching party; whether a political assassi-nation, an internal quarrel among the Chinese, or hostility between the pro-Peking and anti-Peking Chinese; whether the teachers were inculcating the pupils with anticommunist propaganda; or whether the woman became angry because she heard that her son was reprimanded by the teacher for not doing his homework—in Vietnam people had a habit of get-ting hold of a hand grenade, a pistol, an automatic rifle, or gasoline when they got angry—I could never find out the cause. It was a strange coincidence that a funeral home was adjacent to the school, and as I peered at it in passing, shadows of people moved in the dark shop. Coffins painted in vivid red and yellow were piled up to the ceiling, and a baby was sleeping in a new coffin placed under the eaves.

Two days later, I went to an opium den. I heard about it from a young Chinese who was working as an interpreter at the Saigon office of a Japanese newspaper. In the beginning, he was reluctant and tried to frighten me—he said that casual foreign visitors were often stripped completely, or stabbed while asleep and thrown into a canal near the Mytho River—but I gave him enough money to sleep with two girls and forced him to draw a map for me. I went there alone, without telling anyone where I was going. The den was in a congested slum of the Cholon district, and was a hut rather than a house —or even, I should say, a hole in a wall that was colored a rotten green with urine rather than a hut. A rush mat lay on the bare floor and, for some reason, the customers all hung their trousers and shirts on the wall and slept in their shorts. So, the hole looked like the storage closet for a second-hand clothing shop. I made inquiries in my pidgin Vietnamese, and gestured, and a boy wearing a pair of rubber slippers came out and prepared the pipe for me. Some dark, gummy stuff that looked exactly like black shoe polish was in an empty condensed milk can; the boy put some on the tip of a long pin and warmed it up by toasting it over the flame of a lamp. He then put the sizzling substance in the pipe in the shape of a small doughnut, leaving a hole in the middle. In the hovel the destitutes slept like rows of skeletons placed one beside the other, and odors of perspiration and dirt, mingled with smoke, filled the room. A variety of noises came from the men's noses and mouths; their ribs jutted out so clearly that one could

(95

count them, slowly rising and falling as their ghastly, thin bellies also swelled and sank, and their navels moved up and down. The men must have been coolies, stevedores, and rickshaw men. My entire body soon slackened and I fell into a kind of sleep, the flavor of which I could never again remember, no matter how hard I tried. Just before I awoke, I felt a terrible nausea, and I tottered out of the hole to the road.

When I returned to the hotel, I lay down in bed and wondered what I should have for dinner, at the same time feeling that I had had it with the opium. I gradually dozed off on the second wave, which unexpectedly gave me a glimpse of Shangri-la. Nothing with a definite shape appeared and I was in a deep, coma-like sleep; yet my consciousness was crystal clear. The sensation of clarity remains with me even now. There was neither fear, nor irritation—not even pleasure or emotion—but only a pellucid tranquillity. My bones, flesh, inner organs, skin, all vanished, and the sleep was purity itself; there was nothing harsh, only a gentle clarity that expanded soundlessly. There was no space, distance, or direction in this expansion. I felt secure and lost myself in admiration of the lucidity. All the properties of my flesh had evaporated and I had no memory of my eyes having survived, and yet a clear awareness of a visual fascination with translucency distinctly remained with me after I awoke. It was as though I had been sleeping with my eyes open. The completeness of peace and clarity remained with the freshness one feels after a sound sleep, and a soft echo reverberated throughout my body. I remained in bed and listened to the noise of the Saigon night shaking the walls and windows. Until then, I had never experienced rapture without fatigue, but the clearness of the void seemed to have eliminated even that. After this experience, I started looking for words to describe the sleep, but by now I have made its setting seem completely sordid; some-how, however, *"Nenge Mishō"* (a sense of heightened com-munication), an expression I had picked up somewhere, some-time, always remains with me. It may be an insoluble dilemma that I must use words in order to describe a world in which everything is communicable without words; but the fact that I don't hesitate to do so is perhaps an indication that the calm and serene void still remains somewhere in me, unsullied.

She falls to thinking, and then suddenly raises her face and mutters: "I wonder if we are going to a place like that when we die."

Lighting a cigarette I answer, "It would be nice if we were."

She chuckles in a suppressed way: "But I wonder—one can only experience such wonderful feelings when one smokes opium—and supposing one can't—but if it's only those with a taste for filth who can stand a visit to an opium den; I have to be counted out. I feel sick just listening to such a story."

"Filthy is an understatement. It's a cesspool. The pipe-stem has scars made by other teeth and it's all wet with spit and everything from the person who smoked it before. You don't know whether you are inhaling smoke or germs. Just seeing it will make your stomach turn over. But, somehow, in that environment you don't care about it at all, and you stop mind-ing such things. The starting point is about there. That's where we part company."

"I wonder why the second wave of sleep is better both for opium and for alcohol. They both violate the human body. Your brain gets intoxicated and dizzy, so what you have just described—that the second sleep is mild and pleasurable—is because your body is trying to regain an equilibrium after the violation. It must be that; the experience you have described as heightened communication or something or other might be the product of imbalance after fatigue. It must be! When the pendulum swinging to the right is about to return to the left, there is a moment when it seems to stop completely. What you talk about is that blank; that's why it is so serene."

"You seem to be thoroughly familiar with it."

"I wonder if it isn't the feeling of the tide slowly ebbing. A drowned corpse sways leisurely in the shallows. Doesn't it look comfortable and pleasant? Didn't you feel like that corpse?"

"At any rate, it was a masterpiece of sleep. I should call it an exception, because I created it by borrowing the powers of opium, but maybe a sleep cannot be remembered unless it's an exception. It was so vivid and the fact that I can still remember it is remarkable."

"You seem to have many unforgettable memories."

"Not many, but I have some."

"Many things I don't know about."

"Don't say any more."

"Many things I mustn't say."

"I mean, we both have."

"I suppose we do."

After a while, she puts the book face down and leaves. She enters the bright, clean bathroom and brushes her teeth. I turn over lazily on the couch and listen to the sound of water without really listening. She soon comes out and changes into a negligée, dabs one or two drops of Diorissimo on her neck and another on her chin, says goodnight and slips into bed. I pour Schnapps, light a cigarette, and go back mentally to the baby who was sleeping soundly in the coffin, the sizzling sticky paste, and the navels rising and falling on the concave stomachs of the men like hungry demons of Hell.

The reason that I went to an opium den two days after the

incident was because I wanted to prove that blood was blood, smoke was smoke; I was not really trying to erase the memory of blood with smoke. During those two days, I went around asking the police, the information officers of the government, and the American and Vietnamese newspaper reporters whom I knew about the truth behind the incident. But judging from the results, the wasted effort only helped to make the scene fade, burying half its face in the stamp of "Case Unsolved" and changing it from what it was at the moment I witnessed it. I tried to remember the many occasions of bloodshed I had seen in the city, in the frontline jungles, in hospitals, and in the landscape of rice paddies. No matter what the place was, I could not be calm when I saw blood, and, no matter how many times I saw it, I could not get used to it. Blood oppresses me with its disquieting immediacy, whether it has just been flowing, as in the initial stages of coagulation, or has dried. It has an immediacy that I can only stand and look at in a daze. So, I could do nothing but wait for time to pass while I reminisced and compared various incidents. While driving toward the Cholon district in a Renault having a radiator emblem with four horses, a large hole in the floor, and a wire substituting for a door handle, I kept muttering: blood is blood and smoke is smoke. It might have been proof that I was still very much under the influence of the blood. I crawled into the hole in the wall, dragging with me into the den the weight of such well-thumbed concepts as "revolution," "justice," or "Come the Revolution!" Those were words I chewed over every day until I was quite disgusted with them, and yet they did not take me into their confidence, left me on the nebulous periphery. It seemed to me that I had no right to criticize blood in a loud voice unless I was prepared to kill or be killed. And making either preparation meant to write, not in sentences, but in my guts: To kill or be killed. The preparation to be made depended for the most part on one's attitude as to whether one expected anything after the revolution or not; but I was too detached for either. All I could do was watch. If a bullet or shell flew toward me from right or left because I wanted to watch, there was nothing I could do but stand it. I could barely train myself to be prepared to die like a dog.

The scene was extraordinary inside the hole, where there were only pea-sized lamps to light up several spots on the floor, and the boy moped around in the darkness holding the empty milk can, a long pin, and pipes stained with caramel-colored nicotine, but I became accustomed to it in no time. The skinny men, like hungry demons, were dead to the world, lying like patients on operating tables, and their breathing created a busy buzzing throughout the room, suddenly making me feel as though I were in a barber shop or a public bath. After I took off my shirt and trousers and hung them on an old nail on the damp, tacky wall, I lay on a hard mat in my shorts; in the beginning I hesitated, ashamed of my fat body, but as I watched the boy in the dim lamplight preparing the pipe with a thoroughly professional yet somehow sweet gesture, I ceased to worry. The texture of the long bamboo pipes from Laos, on which bits of ivory were inlaid, the boy's flat nose floating in the scanty light, his lively, mischievous eyes, and his placid, expert sluggishness seduced me into a warm reassurance, and the useless soul-searching, which until then had been such a burden, mattered no longer. Gradually, languidly, I merged into the darkness, into the gurgling sounds that were both active and unobtrusive, the darkness filled with snoring and sighs, hesitant yet uncontrollable deep exhalations, the sound of grinding teeth, the salty smell of perspiration, the sour-sweet odor of infected feet, and the peculiar scent of opium. I lost my hands, my abdomen, my shape. I glanced at the face of the man next to me in the light of the miniature lamp. He was truly skin and bone, like the ruthless severity of autumn frost, and ravished by deep wrinkles, but his limbs were stretched long and relaxed, and brilliant blood vessels colored his high cheekbones. I felt relieved when I realized that he was far older than I and that he seemed to be breathing quietly but vigorously, and I was reassured for some reason, thinking that even a man like this visited the den. His wrist, lying on the mat, was emaciated to mere bone, like a thin matchstick. It remained in the corner of my eye, but the sounds soon disappeared, the smells vanished, and so did the walls.

In those days, I knew that I was beginning to fragment and I deliberately overlooked that fact; but more recently, especially now, I can't disregard it any longer. I am half burned out, the adhesive has weathered and lost its viscosity, and I can feel that at the merest touch I would crumble into a multitude of particles and then disperse. Some time ago, in the bar at the station square, early in the morning, she seemed to have said that when one lived in foreign countries for a long time, it was hard to endure the experience of a personality dislocation. I don't think I have enough substance to call a personality, but my dislocation hit me extremely hard. In Tokyo or abroad, when I am walking along a road, I suddenly feel unbearable pain and want to squat; or when I am about to slip through a hotel door, I am shocked to a dead stop; or when I wake up at midnight and stretch my hand to get a lighter, I suddenly freeze. There is no forewarning, no premonition, but unexpectedly it comes and sweeps me off my feet. When I am talking or drinking, I feel an abrupt shock as though I were falling into an abyss. It could be like an avalanche, or a sandy foothold caving in, or legs collapsing all at once, or anything else, but once it occurs, I become idiotically paralyzed. I try desperately to hide the disassociation and show a twisted smile on my face, but the man who has been talking eloquently suddenly turns his eyes away uncertainly, hesitates, or looks bored, so I gather that my eyes have betrayed my condition. I have to hold onto the edge of the table so that my body will not roll off the chair. I am frightened by something enormous that collapses and flees soundlessly from my exterior or my interior, and my eyes must look like those of a child.

Such moments come to me when I am alone, when I am with other people, or when I am in a crowd. They come in a subway concourse in Tokyo, or in a back alley in a foreign country. They come in the midst of eating or love-making. They are whimsical, cruel, merciless, and indiscriminate. Once they attack me, I am overpowered and everything is in pieces until they leave. Conversation, jokes, wit, smiles, words, all are swept off instantly and sucked into a dust funnel. There is not even time to cry out, "Wait!" When I sense the moment, it is already always after the fact, and I stand in frozen stupor, in the soundless, odorless devastation of a riverbed, looking around me. Or I feel that the bottles, the dishes, the fat cheeks of the chef, the shiny glass doors, and the gigantic buildings beyond them are nothing but magnificent and heartless trash, irredeemable waste, and I stand petrified like an immigrant on the wharf who had just gotten off the ship.

For the past ten years I have done nothing but travel. As I lie on the sofa contemplating and absorbing Schnapps like a slovenly sponge, I begin to think I have only been fleeing wildly in those moments, and while intending always to be one step ahead, I was always ambushed and beaten to the ground. I surrendered without a fight and roamed in aimless craving and fear. The beginning of a journey is sure to excite me, but while driving on the dark highway to the airport I already feel the fire going out. On the return home, I have a single-minded desire for Japanese tea, buckwheat noodles, seaweed, and chilled bean curd, but there is almost nothing else. Rather, distaste and melancholy drift on the edge of nothingness. My instability is evident in the fact that I began to loll on the couch all day only a few days after I came to this glass room. Furthermore, there is nothing distinguished about departure or return; nevertheless, some three months later I am already beginning to feel restless. I begin to resent this sedimentation. I feel as if I am slowly rotting away from the head down. Regardless of my motivation, traveling is, ultimately, a journey through myself, using the foreign land as a catalyst; but a journey having myself as the goal will sooner or later arrive at a terrible void. Am I not just stuffing a vacuum with meat, bread, and alcohol every day?

It would be easier if I could think that I have become blasé because I have traveled too much. But the moment of disassociation seems to have the same intensity now, at forty, as it did when I was eighteen, regardless of whether I am traveling or not. Ever since my childhood I have always been suddenly attacked by the unnameable and felt frozen or crushed. I could not possibly feel excited or passionate while I was afraid of collapsing at some unexpected moment. I was frightened of passion, but I also feared being awakened from it. I could not touch anything when I thought of the moment of attack in the midst of exhilaration. I always needed a dark room somewhere where no one's eyes could reach. I required a small, quiet chamber into which I could creep the moment it happened, where I could doze while waiting for all the pieces to return and resume the shape of an effigy with a heart marked "I." Sometimes, the moment crushed and swept away even that small chamber in its destructive momentum; then I walked around aimlessly, whether it was night or day, until my chin dropped on my chest. Or I had to go into one movie house after another, and after seeing a few minutes of each film, I would leave and go on to another; after sampling seven theaters I entered still another. The daylight and the darkness fused together like a completely disordered sentence without punctuation or grammar, and I lost the energy even to feel troubled, but I had to exhaust myself until my knees began to shake. It was like the hopeless task of superimposing colors and waiting to see whiteness appear, but while flying from darkness to daylight, daylight to darkness, like a bat in the daytime, while I knew I was wallowing in lethargy, I sometimes wondered whether I wasn't really a passionate, frenzied enthusiast.

In order to hold onto myself, with my habit of collapsing before a momentary attack more easily than a house of cards, or to put myself together again, perhaps I should have used my hands. Breaking objects, making them, or even touching them would have helped. I should have used my hands. I should have followed the teachings of the ancient Chinese philosopher who preached using the hands even if it were only for gambling, or the Indian philosopher who soaked his fingers in water and concentrated on internal monologues. But I did not have enough energy to go off and look for a pasture or a factory, and I didn't know when or where those moments would occur. I abused my eyes by entering movie theaters I happened to pass. By creeping into the darkness that was constantly changing color and sound, filled with the rustling of breath and flabby, warm skins that gave off unpleasant odors, I could momentarily escape the ebbing, flowing force. Then, mixed with a fear both burning and vague, a small bit of warm reassurance began to seep in. In the light of much later times, as I think about those days when I sank into the darkness of the opium den, as black as the storage room of a second-hand clothing shop, and stretched my body full length,

I realize that what drove me in my teens, twenties, and thirties is still pursuing me.

On leaving the movie theater, if it is still daytime, I feel a terrible shock as soon as I am exposed to the outside light. It is like a kick from behind. In a familiar environment like Shinjuku or Yuraku-cho, the customary signboards and buildings attract my eyes and give me a definite, although hollow, shape; but in an unfamiliar neighborhood like Gotanda or Kōtō, I feel as helpless as if I had landed on a strange planet, even though I am unmistakably in Tokyo. The deformation does not stop but eats further into me. I feel easier at night, no matter where. I feel the loneliness, but it fits me like old clothes, which I can wear like a freshly laundered and revitalized shirt; it is almost invigorating.

A comedy, a tragedy, a Western, a domestic drama, a farce, a musical, a cartoon, the story of an exploration, a war film, a documentary. While looking up at the marquee and weighing the amount of my remaining energy, I enter the darkness. But at the slightest provocation in dialogue or scene, I am unnerved; I stand up, and again hurriedly enter another theater. I absorb bits of sighs, chuckles, the clicking of tongues, voiceless sneering, sudden guffaws, from all the faceless people, and I turn into a toy box full of dialogues, visions, and scenes, as I trudge along the soiled pavement. They are mere scraps, but intense dialogues and poignant lines boil inside me, and I turn into a stew pot. I receive suggestions, I feel gorged and frightened by the hack work of the screenplay writers who slash down an enormous substance into a single word. I clack my tongue and catch the last train to the suburbs. I am exhausted and can hardly breathe, but the trauma of being pushed out into the broad daylight from the dark is not there. Rather, the pale desolation of the old iron boxes filled with drunken men, drunken women, others who can't get drunk, sluttish girls, lethargic youths, the bubbles and juice of vomit, trash like that at a race track, suits me; nothing is more appropriate than a midnight train filled with trash and noise. Everyone has lost the energy needed to cover themselves up, and so they remain exposed; their eyes turning into those of fish or frogs, they stare unashamedly, without avoiding one another's glances. Crumpled pages of the newspaper's sports section cast a fortress-like shadow on the floor.

When the political power shift, as fleeting as swaying gossamer, was taking place in Saigon, a foreign reporter pointed it out to the information officer—who in turn answered, with a calm look—that things were the same in the time of the French Revolution. This episode offered food for conversation that night among the reporters on the cocktail circuit. Whether to laugh at this answer or not depended on one's knowledge of history, and how much one was involved in the fate of this country, but the reporters in general sneered cynically at the remark, mainly for the reason that it was anachronistic. Panting in the humid heat that could probably squeeze oily perspiration out of completely dry bones, I was sipping a martini that had lost its sharp edge, and was laughing perfunctorily, but at least trying to make my barbs cutting enough. The fact that I could be serious about anachronisms that happened all the time in my own country but could offer only sarcasm and wit about those that happened in a distant foreign one only proved how indifferent I was about Vietnam.

One day I went with a Japanese reporter to see the prime minister at his official residence. The question time was extremely limited, and the reporter alone was permitted to ask questions; it was stipulated that I keep silent. After a series of questions, the reporter asked an extremely pointed one:

"Do you think the use of a nuclear bomb is permissible in order to end this war?"

The prime minister, having listened to the interpreter's translation, fell into a bovine silence, hunching his thick neck. Later it became evident that he was in power for only eighty or ninety days, but by anyone's standard, he was a man of integrity, purity, and fortitude. In the midst of corruption, he was never stained by it, and in the days of Diem, although he shared the same principles, he experienced the misery of exile to the Poulo Condor Islands; in times of misfortune he was said to have worked as a tricycle driver and a typist, and was reported to have no peer in integrity, at least. In appearance, he was a gross village chief. His neck, hands, and chest were thick, and his eyes did not flash with wit or cunning; everything about him was bucolic, heavy, and dull. He had somewhat the air of having been suddenly awakened from his siesta in a distant village surrounded by rice paddies and banana groves in order to assume the prime minister's office, embodying mud, heavy taxes, and endless toil.

He answered in a grave voice: "If the entire world agrees to use the bomb, I will."

This anticommunist, who was poor and upright, who seemed to live only for his convictions, muttered this without showing any spark of fanatical passion. I looked in a daze at the mass of wrinkles on his strong, sun-tanned neck. Presumably he had forged his merciless, uncompromising attitude in the prison of an isolated island, or glued to the tricycle handles, or in the soporific, monotonous sounds of the typewriter, all of which I had never known, and I felt that he was speaking out of his deliberations through night and day, after vacillating in his opinions and observing his enemies. Later, when I was told that he was exiled by third-class actors who were much younger than he, I found out that the reason was his almost obstinate honesty and uprightness.

But what I felt then, in the humid heat, sitting on the sofa, was the feeling of a formless, sweaty disassociation. I had not really touched on the determination of this village master, who stated distinctly, although in a low voice, that he could consent to the use of a nuclear bomb only if the entire world agreed to do so.

Without any denial, affirmation, fondness, hatred, anything, I continued to stare at the profile of the placid man, my eyes wide open. I was looking at the deep wrinkles of his neck as though I were gazing into the shadows of a newspaper on the last train from Tokyo. I had no way of judging whether he was speaking habitual lines in diplomatic language, or wishing to express the passion and thoroughness of his own conviction. I only knew that I had no love, hatred, resentment, contempt, sympathy, fear, none of these things, not even a speck of feeling. I was overpowered by his air of lifelong hardship, the bitter secretion of which oozed from his body, and by his painful experiences, which I would never be able to go through even in a million years. On the other hand, in that room with the broken air conditioner, annoyed by the flood of perspiration, I was overburdened with myself, and as slack as a piece of rubber rotted by the cold.

Summer festers on.

Summer has become diseased rather than ripe. Early in the morning, the chirping of birds is heard from the direction of the forest, and the sunlight is filled with buoyant excitement. But it lasts only until about ten o'clock, and after that the sky is filmed with a white sheen and soft-membraned clouds appear everywhere. I leave the door to the balcony completely open, but the breeze slackens and stagnates like lukewarm water, and there is none of the sword-blade fresh-ness that was there a short while ago. A large shadow forms behind the curtain, and I roll myself in it like a crab crawling into a hole, but there is none of the coolness to be found in a deep pool. All through the long afternoon, the transparent shimmer of red-hot coal fills the room. After my afternoon nap, I get up for a shower. While the water runs down my skin, I recover my shape, but I begin to melt as soon as I return to the couch. All I can do is to travel between the couch and the bathroom through the hot, dense, shimmering air.

On the sofa, which, a packhorse no longer, is now even more miserably crumpled and limp, I continue to perspire and turn into a melting lump of butter. The pizza, which she bakes wearing her bra, wiping off her perspiration as she kneads the dough, is full of rich nourishment, starch, fat, and protein, and as I carry it piece by piece to my mouth, I feel that the dough is adding soft flesh to my belly; the anchovies giving bags to my cheeks; and the salami adding a bulging pouch to my chest. When I finish the meal and get up, my perspiring body is much heavier, and I feel as if my body is loaded with cumbersome burdens.

"Ingest and defecate, ingest and defecate. It's just like a lugworm or earthworm. It's the security of an earthworm. Pure consumption. No eyes, no ears, only get fat and there are no complaints. Sweet indolence. I wonder if *dolce vita* ulti-mately means to get fat."

"It doesn't matter, does it? I don't mind. I'm happy if you get fat on what I cook. Don't fret. You're on vacation now; all you have to do is eat and sleep in my shadow and get fat. I'll fatten you up so that you won't be able to escape. I'm delighted. I feel like a mother cat."

"How is the town?"

"Fewer people every day. The liquor and grocery stores

are closing fast, and finding food is not easy. The store that was open yesterday is closed and locked today, and the sign says, 'We'll be away for three weeks.' The paper says that twenty million people will leave for vacation this year. It's a record-breaking figure, they say. All the roads both north and south are jam-packed, and in some spots traffic came to a complete halt for four hours the day before yesterday. Judging from this, we may see twenty-five million vacationers next summer, and break the records again. Of course, it's only the newspapers that are getting excited about it; people don't seem to pay any attention."

"How is Professor Steinkopf?"

"All three have gone separate ways. Herr Professor went to the mountains, his wife went to the shore, and the secretary to an unknown destination. The student who told me about it is also leaving for somewhere today; the campus and the whole seminar room have emptied. The students' movement disappeared into thin air a long time ago. Someone was saying that he was going to spend the summer at the shore healing his bruises and his scars from police-dog bites, and the students are going to fight again in the fall. I wonder. Vacation flushes away everything."

"Are we the only ones staying?"

"Along with the railroad workers."

Her reply was instantaneous and, on her lips, hiding behind her laughter, was etched the sharp wrinkle of a sneer. Until recently, it had been a mere shade drifting on the boundaries of resignation and patience, but each day has made it sharper and more overt lately.

Food and memories have increased my weight. Remembrances have turned into excess fat, which hangs sloppily from various parts of my body. Since I handle these recollections every day, they are soiled with fingerprints, the forms and faces completely obliterated. Yet when I fall onto the couch or rise from it, or when I sit at the table for meals, I am tempted to feel that my body has grown heavy with memories. I am an old warehouse filled with unclaimed bales that are misshapen, half spilled, half rotten, almost evaporating, on which the dates of shipment and the senders' addresses have been blurred—I am such an old warehouse, and yet I want to feel like a ship the day before it leaves on a voyage. As in the days when I was waiting for her in the room with the worn-out red curtains, passing the time sleeping and waking, a strange flaccid thing is beginning to grow out of my body. It is taking root, extending its stems, spreading leaves, and waving tendrils. It has entrapped me, forcing me down onto the couch so that I cannot move, and then has overflowed onto the floor, creeping over the carpet, slowly proliferating, covering the yak hide, and now it is trying to cover the entire wall. Rustling and breathing heavily, it is about to pin me down to the sofa and cover my entire body. If I sit up, it hesitates and vanishes momentarily, but as I cross the room, go to the bathroom, and turn the shower handle, it is already encroaching there too. It starts to envelop me from my head down, spreads silently around my shoulders and my belly, and, then, rustling, it starts to crawl up the shinbones to the thigh. When the cold water spurts over my head, it retreats briefly; but as the liquid warms and flows down my head, shoulders, chest, abdomen, testicles, and thighs, it gets more and more of a hold, trying to imprison me. I am a room; a hollow room. There is no man, no light, and yet luxuriant vines cover the wall.

It was the day before yesterday.

About four in the afternoon, I was still drowsy after a nap, but my eyelids felt the incandescent heat swelling in the room, and I remained in a stupor, with my eyes closed. Suddenly the bell rang in the wall by the door, and a low, husky man's voice was heard. There had been no visitors since I had come here, and although I knew that such a device as the bell existed, I had never heard it actually ring. The man's voice was firm, efficient, and friendly. He called her name two or three times, and said something in the language of this country, which I did not understand. The woman, who had been sleeping snuggled against the opposite wall, jumped out of bed and, snatching the intercom, shouted in a high voice. She talked fast, bubbling over with loud laughter and soft exclamations. After some conversation, she put her hands on her bare hips and looked at me. Her eyes sparkled with vivacity and a gay animation that I had not seen for a long time.

Smiling, she said, "Professor Schwarzenberg has come back from America. It's an impressive name but it has nothing to do with the Schwarzenbergstrasse in Vienna. He was a professor of mathematics at the University, but he couldn't get along there and went to a university in America. He says he's coming up now. We used to have pizza parties every so often in this room. He's a mathematician but a real peasant. He goes to the woods and cuts trees and splits them with an ax to build himself a house. He doesn't feel right unless he does it that way. Naturally, he disagreed with the administration on everything and went to the United States. He loves to fish and I think you'll get along with him. He is just dropping in to say hello. He's coming right up. It's been two years."

As she was saying all this she dashed over to her bed, seized a shirt from the floor, and, with a twist of her body, thrust her legs into denim pants. Then she ran over to the mirror on the wall, tidied her hair, and sprayed on perfume.

"Please! Don't just lie there!" she shouted in her elation.

While I was lazily picking myself up off the couch, a vague gloom began to spread, and before I could control it, it pervaded my whole body. I wrapped my bare torso with a blanket and got off the couch, and after smoothing out the wrinkles, went into the kitchen. Behind me, the bell rang sharply and the voice of a middle-aged man was heard. Her voice welcomed him excitedly. He seemed to sit down on the couch and a gay conversation started. I was holding my breath during all of this, looking at the vague, misty reflection of my face on the kettle. She had thoroughly polished it, along with the frying pans, and dishes, and the kitchen was spotless, with no odor, no shadows; everything was shining with the hygienic cleanliness of a hospital. She was talking constantly, asking questions and answering, laughing loudly all the while. She seemed to have opened up extrovertly, and her voice was notably exhilarated. Listening to it, I realized how much she had suppressed because of me.

The depth of her depression was marked by her very buoyancy now. It was as though a nurse had suddenly rediscovered her womanhood after working hours. Bitterness slowly began to infiltrate me. An ungainly stiffness pervaded my body, and I was overtaken by impalpable disgust and fear. I was embittered and depressed by my feebleness in not having the energy to exchange greetings with one simple university professor. While looking at the kettle, I held the blanket so that it would not fall from my hips, but I felt that I lacked the strength to lift a finger, or to take a step, and that I could not possibly leave the kitchen. Stifling heat was quivering against the walls and I was standing there, perspiring. Resentment rose from the wall, from the tap, the dishes, spoons, bottles, from the very orderliness of the rows and arrangements of these objects, and corroded the entire area like a strong acid.

She stood at the kitchen doorway and spoke.

"There you are! I was wondering where you were, and you were hiding here. Just look at you, you do look funny! Come out."

"Did the Professor leave?"

"He went home. He wanted to talk to you about fishing. He said he was sorry he couldn't meet you, but he would come back again. He's a little eccentric but a nice person. Please meet him the next time. I think you will get along nicely. You can relax with him."

I started to say something and fell silent. Whatever the Professor had left behind him was shining and swaying gently in her face, and her whole expression was alive. She looked like a prisoner who had received a passionate letter. She was excited enough to start dancing. She was not yet aware of the fact that I had turned to mere refuse. She either did not feel it or refused to recognize it. I slipped past her with the blanket still around my hips and rolled onto the couch. An unfamiliar wrinkle and dent had already formed, but as soon as I fell into it, my shape reappeared and effortlessly absorbed my weight. As soon as I breathed once or twice, I became a flabby mass of fat once again, and I felt a premonition of tangled, twisted, abundant leafy vines burying my body and covering my face. The strength that had been beginning to sprout from my renewed activity immediately withered.

After eating macaroni for supper, we took deck chairs onto the balcony, as usual; we stretched out and ate some cherries. The familiar violet-red-purple was beginning to spread over the sky, but I was still shot through with the incandescent heat of the long and drowsy afternoon and I could hardly breathe. I felt as if the room behind me were filled with perspiration, body odor, and poison. I was crushed in the deck chair, feeling that even to lift my hand and spit the cherry stones into it, one by one, was too great a risk.

I wonder what started it all; while we were stretched out lazily on the deck chairs chatting, she began to get upset for some reason. At first, it was the usual small talk mixed with banter, but I was not responding satisfactorily; while she did most of the talking, her tone started to take on a note of irrepressible acrimony, intensified by what she was actually saying, and she began to rear her head like a snake.

"They say that if a bespectacled Oriental comes down the street with a camera hanging from his shoulder, you can be sure that he's Japanese. But in my opinion, it's the way they walk. I can tell them at a glance, from the way they walk. For some reason, the Yamato race is not good at walking. They are extremely poor walkers. Not only poor, but really ugly. I can't tell why, but their walk is hopelessly inelegant. I can't stand it, and want to look away. You can tell from three blocks away, and you say to yourself, there comes a Yamato. I feel like running away into an alley. I wonder if I walk like that, being one myself, and I am appalled. I hear these days that instructions for sexual gymnastics are given in women's magazines, complete with photographs; if they are that thorough, why don't they teach their readers to walk? But worse than the ugly walk is their eyes. They have a repulsive, absolutely off-putting look. They are peculiarly timid and arrogant at the same time. I think really confident people are rather modest, but the Yamatos are the reverse. That's it—they have a frightened look about them and yet they are filled with pride. This is especially true of the intellectuals. If they go to a restaurant, they sit in a corner as if glued to the wall, and they don't feel safe unless they're with other Japanese. Somehow a Yamato seems to be very insecure when he's alone and this is not just true of country bumpkins; those newspapermen and scholars who sneer at them behave in exactly the same way. Japanese newspapermen always tend to congregate, and the same faces eat at the same restaurant every day, don't they? Some of them sound clever when they say that they will become rootless if they don't continue to speak Japanese, and they must write in their own language; but that's a lie. The truth is that they can't function alone. So, you will notice, all the overseas news items in the Japanese papers are more or less the same. Their sources are friends who swap information, like exchanging tips at a brokerage house, and most items are rewrites of articles that have appeared in foreign newspapers. It's preposterous. These Japanese are called 'newspaper reporters' because they report the news that has already been printed in other papers. The reporters here laugh at them. I know it because I have some acquaintances among them; Japanese newspapermen have become a laughingstock. Yet they don't know it. They console each other by swapping petty 'inside' slander that can be understood by no one else. But the minute one of them leaves, the others begin talking about him. His back is hardly turned before they start gossiping, and, until that minute, he had been talking and laughing with them. Of course it's not only the reporters, but the scholars and businessmen as well; they're all the same. I think they are deplorable. Scholars are especially unbearable. They dash off a translation of an essay that has appeared in a journal here; all they do is change the language and transcribe the horizontal writing into vertical writing and publish it. And if the essay happens to touch the core of a timely problem and ride the mood of Japanese mass media, the transcriber becomes a scholar in the limelight overnight. You can't beat the slickness of it. While they are over here, what do they do? Like the others, they stick together as Japanese and they talk about one another surreptitiously, that's all. They can't challenge the native scholars here in a head-on battle to win a logical victory; they can't possibly do that. Since this is the case, when they return to Japan and write an essay, they should be modestly discreet—that would have some redeeming grace; but they pretend that they have waged great verbal battles and they sound as if what they are publishing is the outcome of a great controversy. Besides, when they rewrite horizontal sentences into vertical sentences, the result is full of mistranslations, unintentionally funny translations, and plain bad translations. What can you do? Of course, there are some unreliable essays too, but the unreliability in this country bears no comparison to that of the Japanese. An eminent Kyoto University authority on Chinese literature, who is held in great awe, made a speech in Chinese and it was completely unintelligible to the Chinese; and again, an extremely prominent scholar of English from a university in Tokyo spoke at a Shakespearean Society meeting in London or somewhere, and nobody understood a word . . . Well, all this makes one start to think. Is there one specialist among the Yamatos who is sufficiently devoted to a foreign language to write his diary in that language? I've never heard of such a one since Tenshin Okakura.*A specialist should be able to devote himself to his subject to that extent. A Shakespearean scholar should write his diary in Shakespearean English."

As the dusk crept in, she continued to cram her mouth with cherries, spitting out stones, and chattering in her irritated, bitterly sneering tone of voice. I believe that once a snake has raised its head, it strikes only once to inflict a mortal wound, but she held hers high, swayed, and struck at one subject after another as they came up and bit every one of them. And each time she retreated to prepare herself for the next attack, when she struck again more vehemently than ever. She began to look as if the venom she kept for the enemy

---

*A Meiji period philosopher and art historian (1862–1913), who rediscovered Japanese art with Ernest Fenollasa. [*trans.*]

was affecting her. The fever from her own poison had not yet broken out perceptibly, but a tone of intoxication was already there. After cursing Japanese travelers, newspapermen, and scholars, she ranted at the touring peasants who swaggered through hotel corridors in their underwear. She raged at Japanese "gentlemen" who begin telling bawdy jokes as soon as they have one drink and who (in a brothel) shrink at the sight of a white woman's naked body, and yet like to talk big. She fumed at the tourists who are ready to present *ukiyoe* stamps and *kokeshi* dolls indiscriminately to hotel bellboys or cigarette girls in cabarets or to anyone at all. She seethed at the fact that Italian cameo sellers break into big smiles as soon as they see a Japanese and call out *"Moshi moshi kameo kamesan yo."* ["Hello little turtle, hello, hello!"] She attacked the embassy personnel who fill their homes with the reeking smell of strong Japanese pickles and yet insult Limburger cheese. She cursed Tokyo, with its population of more than ten million and no capacity for treating sanitary waste, sixty to seventy percent of which is dumped in the ocean, while the city is engrossed in building more highways and skyscrapers. She cursed reporters, scholars, and writers who criticize Japan and the Japanese. She stormed at the translators, publishers, the newspaper press, the right wing, the left wing, and she ranted at Japan and the Japanese in relation to everything she could think of.

Behind the venomous, cutting edge of these imprecations, there was an unmistakable air of loneliness. As I listened, I could finally guess, though vaguely, what had sustained her through these past ten years, about which I knew nothing. The girl who could not live in Japan except as a *ku ai tsu*, and yet who was too proud to surrender and had therefore established herself as an exile, probably had no other choice but to live as an orphan here too. She must have lived on the strength she drew from her hatred of Japan and the Japanese. She must have survived the annihilating early mornings and the frightful but intimate evenings, exuding hatred, the way a shell exudes lime. Working as an interpreter for a touring group, or a dishwasher at a restaurant, or a cigarette girl at a cabaret, or a typist at a Japanese commercial firm, she had eked out a living. The hatred that burst open and poured out so breathlessly was a result of the hands that had almost dissolved in detergent, the stereotyped routine comments that had almost frozen her lips, the thick fog of smoke that had nearly constricted her throat, and the rough walls of the desolate toilet. It must also have risen from the leftover meals consisting of fat meat covered with crushed cigarette stubs or fish that had become completely cold. The slimy simpering wet eyes in the darkness, the gigantic worm-like white fingers taking out a wallet, the thick lips glistening with saliva, and the roar of cymbals filled with hollow passion— while all these things beat against her and almost broke her, she somehow tenaciously withstood them all and lived on in the garret, cultivating her hate.

We had been sitting in the evening afterglow, and now night had fallen unnoticed. The rays of the setting sun finally faded from the sky and from the balcony, and a hint of coolness to come stirred from time to time. Undaunted, she continued to spew vulgarity and spite at the dark rather than at me in a voice that was shrill, though under control, her head held high.

"That's enough; quite enough," I muttered when she stopped for breath. The touch of the hard, coarse canvas of the deck chair felt chilly and pleasant on the skin, but I felt dully obese and a disagreeable half-rancid fatty acid coursed through my body.

"I envy you for being able to hate Japan that much. You have survived on the strength of that alone. The problem is what happens from now on. You will receive your doctorate; I'm sure you will get it. I don't know anything about your dissertation, but I believe you will. When you become a doctor, you will avenge yourself magnificently on Japan. Then, what will you do after that? You won't be able to hate Japan as much as you did in the past, because once your ambitions are achieved your passionate need for hatred will die. You will be sobered. When your intoxication cools, living will be difficult. How does that strike you? Is there something else that you can lose yourself in, something that you can be infatuated with?"

Suddenly she seemed to inhale deeply in the darkness and stiffen as though under attack. I both liked and pitied her sensitivity. Inadvertently I had asked her questions I should have been asking myself. In the momentary silence that followed her venomous harangue, her fear was palpable.

After a while, I murmured, "I have nothing."

She caught her breath and barely whispered, "I don't either."

Soon she stood up from the lounge chair and went silently inside; she did not return. When I went in dragging my physical encumbrances, she was sitting on the couch, gazing into the yak fur at her feet. Her face was pale, her eyes hollow, and her lips a little parted. I took out a bottle of Schnapps from the refrigerator and poured two glasses. They immediately clouded with white frost, but she did not move to reach for one.

Slowly she muttered: "You are cruel. You said horrible things. You dug out things I had suppressed and was afraid to expose. You not only pointed them out but you also suddenly destroyed my very foundations. It was like knocking over a stool while I was standing on it on my tiptoes, trying to reach up for something. Your intuition is impressive but you are too inhuman."

"I didn't mean it."

"I know. You wanted me to shut up. People are all like that. When I start abusing Japan, they all turn away. Even the people who have been just as abusive as I am fall silent. There must be something unpleasant about me, some odor. I don't recognize my own body odor so I get carried away, but it must be disagreeable. Sometimes I come to my senses and then even I want to turn away. Living alone in a place like this, I've turned into such a horrible person. As you say, there was nothing I could lean on but my hatred of Japan. I hated it from A to Z. All I could do was hate Japan, and I ran through life like a horse with blinders. It hit me hard when you asked me what I would do when my hatred subsided. That's exactly it. I sometimes wonder about it and shudder. I don't show it in front of other people, but I suddenly feel as if I had been pushed over a cliff. I feel paralyzed and drugged into a daze somehow. It's terrible, I feel that I am rolling over and over, falling down into my own body. I'm afraid."

She raised her face slowly, and looked vacantly around the room. She stared as if she had grown old and wan all at once. A long wrinkle as clearly as a scar formed around her mouth. She hunched back, let her shoulders droop, and seemed to shrink; her broad, white back and voluptuous hips lost their usual impact, and she seemed as totally helpless as a child. She had closed up, frozen as she had never done before, but at least she was not shattered. She seemed to be suffering the premonitions of a breakdown. In contrast to her own air of bleakness, the surrounding atmosphere suddenly seemed almost choking.

"I washed dishes, sold cigarettes, made love, and traveled. I wore black silk stockings and walked around like a bunny girl, selling cigarettes, with a wooden box hanging from my neck. But according to the handyman at the cabaret, my face was tragic. The customers probably felt depressed when they saw me. I had ardent love affairs. It's not necessary to tell you how many but at least they were passionate. There were two men who made me think about marriage; I pondered over it night after night. They were both scholars, but not Japanese. They were not without sorrows, but they had substance as well and they were serious. But, ultimately, I could not take the final step. In those days, I had been awarded a scholarship and I went back to being a student again. I was all ambition to do from the start what I couldn't do in Japan, and I was overcome by my feeling of not wanting to lose my freedom. At least that is what I told myself. Each said that I could go on studying after marriage and they would cooperate, but I was drunk, infatuated with the freedom that I had finally seized. Until then, I had been bent only on destroying myself; now, unexpectedly, I had saved myself, and I was intoxicated. I didn't want to throw away my freedom on marriage, and I didn't want to spoil it. But there are a lot of things I feel helpless about these days—not money or earning a living, I don't have to worry about that, but as I said before, I often feel lonely and want a child or something. I had never even thought about a baby; I had decided to ignore such things completely; but when I am alone at night, typing, I begin suddenly to crave a baby. The thought becomes unbearable when I start to imagine how it would be if I had a child now. I begin to think I might be deformed in some way. It's silly. I had made up my mind that I would protect my freedom, and I had sworn that I would desert both Japan and marriage to keep it. I have been saying, as you always did, that you have to lose something in order to gain something; but now, at my age, I have begun to feel differently, and when it gets bad I feel that I don't care who the man is, anyone will do, a test-tube baby will do. I don't mind having artificial insemination or an illegitimate child. I was one. I don't care. Whatever it is, it doesn't bother me. I can do it; look at me, I've lived through everything until now."

Suddenly tears gushed from her wide eyes and began to stream down her cheeks. She clenched her fists resting on her pale, sinewy knees and let the tears flow freely. After holding herself like this for a while, she suddenly fell prostrate on the couch. After the flood abated, she began to cry more quietly, the sobs shaking her shoulders and abdomen from time to time. She beat the couch silently but intently with her fists as if ashamed of her breakdown.

She moaned: "I want a baby, I want it, now!"

I didn't move. I muttered two or three words, but they were no consolation, no help, or encouragement. They surged up from my cold, troubled heart, but when they left my lips they were already turned to vague nothings that vanished immediately. Words with any shape or meaning, words with any quantity could not possibly be drawn from me now, no matter how I shook myself. I sat at the table and folded my arms like a quack doctor, casting stealthy glances alternately at the glass of Schnapps and at her profile. Some part of me seemed to be calculating that I should not open my mouth too carelessly, but even this awareness was nothing that I could feel involved in, or rack my brains over. I just sat there, cold, lethargic, dazed, and uncomfortable. I was rather envious of her physical surrender to remorse. It moved me to something like awe. I began to feel ashamed that I had been so reluctant to enter or touch her heart and yet had devoured her body. Feeling neither anger nor alienation, I just drifted, inept.

After a while, she stopped crying and wiped the tears

from her cheeks and chin with her fist. She stared at the tiny, soft wrinkles of the leather on the couch. Her eyes were dreamy and her voice hushed but insolent.

"When I left Japan, only Toki came to say goodbye. She came to the Yokohama harbor to give me a send-off. I had no furniture or other movable belongings, but I left what little I had with the landlady and Toki. For some reason, I got along with her. She is lucky, she got married and has two or three babies by now. It took me ten years just to become a student again, but she has already given birth to children, one after another, without any trouble at all. She sends me photographs sometimes. Children in this country are adorable, as bubbly as champagne. But Japanese children are lovable too. Their eyes and nose are so tiny and their hair is jet black and straight. They are like little arrowheads or *kokeshi* dolls. I think it must feel wonderful to hold them. Then I lose all sense of proportion. I feel their dewy, downy, soft, firm weight in my arms. They lean on me completely for support and need me totally. That breaks my heart. If I had a child like that, I wouldn't care about its father. He could roam all he wanted to and talk about his wife behind her back and sleep around. Fathers are not needed. I have some training in abstract logic, so I don't care whose child it is. Wait and see—I'll become an earth mother. I'm sure of it. I'll take the semen of some man I don't know from Adam and conceive a baby. I'll wheel the baby in a pram and take him to the park, and I'll knit woollen socks or read him the old-fashioned poems of Blok and sometimes I'll even say 'koochi koochi koo' to that child of nature. I won't care if he grows up and deserts me. I'll give myself to him completely. I'll become devotion personified. I can't help myself. The saying 'a mother is both ugly and beautiful' will apply to me. You like my belly because it has no wrinkles, but it is seedless, barren. You've never thought about that, have you?"

She slowly got up from the couch, picked up the Schnapps glass with her little finger crooked, and took a sip. She grimaced, as though clicking her tongue, then changed expression and went into the bathroom. After a while she came out, and a faint fragrance of Diorissimo wafted past; looking up, I saw her eyes shine darkly. She suddenly flashed the disintegrating hedgehog under my nose and threw it over on the table, then shouted, half as a threat and half as a sneer: "Koochi koochi koo!"

Breathing hard, she added with dignity: "That's all I have!"

Suddenly she let out a strange cry, dashed over to the couch, and fell on it; she began to pound the leather, striking out with her fists as she writhed and burst into tears. She wept loudly, as if her unrestrained cries were being wrung from her very body. It was as if a bright, shining glass box had suddenly shattered with a deafening crack. This room, the very embodiment of the elaboration and perfection of modern technology, was nothing but a primeval forest to her. She wailed and twisted on the couch; she abandoned herself to unadulterated grief, with great heaving sobs. As her voice rose and fell, I felt its hard impact all over my body, like concrete, and I stood distracted, holding the glass of Schnapps; I felt like a fool. I thought of escaping to the balcony but somehow couldn't. So I looked at her hair, which parted and closed with each attack of sobbing. I felt as though I were standing under the dark night sky, completely naked. An intense desolation, stronger than anything I had experienced, overpowered me and I staggered. The suffocating growth that had twisted and twined around me disappeared.

"Shall we go somewhere?" I said, vaguely.

We went to a mountain lake. "Bucktail" means the tail of a deer, but sometimes the artificial fly made with hair from a buck's tail is also given this name. Hooks are usually covered with various bird feathers, but this one is made with animal fur: deer tail, polar bear hair, squirrel tail, or goat hair. Mostly, natural colors are used, but sometimes the hairs are tinted various shades. First, one buys a long-stemmed hook and wraps the shaft in red or yellow braid and binds it with gold or silver thread. Then one attaches a handful of multicolored fur to the neck of the hook with silk thread and fixes it with glue. As the hook is pulled through the water, the fur hairs open and close like flowers. The deciding factor in one's selection of the color of the fur is the specific color of the water.

Hooks that are made to look like fish food, such as insects, larvae, and small fish, are called "imitators"; those that attract fish only by means of color, flashes of metal, and quivering movements are called "attractors." I am hoping to catch pike; they are omnivorous tyrants that gulp down anything that crosses their path, whether it has wings, fur, scales, no scales, anything. Therefore the hook that attracts them can be either an imitator or an attractor. I went with her to a fishing tackle shop and, after buying various materials for artificial flies, I bought a very cheap rod and reel for beginners. I also bought spinners. I thought of removing the three hooks that are normally attached to them and substituting my own bucktails and trying some casting. I was going to use the spinners in place of a weight; since they are not like ordinary sinkers and have rotary propellers, they will spin in the water and create flashes of light. They might help to make the hooks more effective by increasing the vibration of the hairs. If the place has not already been ransacked by other fishermen, the unsophisticated fish hiding in the reeds or under the water lilies in the lake will not know that objects leaving small eddies and flashes can be something other than food or dead leaves. So . . .

I wanted to catch trout but it is not the season; besides, fly-casting rods are expensive, and I hesitated to buy one. Pike are easy to catch, but the best season for them is spring or autumn. When there's nothing to catch, no equipment will help. The proprietor of the shop, who had strong shoulders and a thick chest, kindly told me about four or five lakes that supplied good pike fishing in this season; I bent over a map with a red pencil in my hand and tried to discover the best one, by checking the land level, the topography, whether it was fed by rivers, or surrounded by tourists, taking all possible factors into account. Pike are solitary creatures—gloomy, greedy, lone wolves—and their mouths are all teeth; some people even say that their tongues have teeth and that their taste buds are not on their tongues but in their throats. By nature they prefer cold water, so I had to pick a lake in a high-altitude area or on a plateau, given that it was now midsummer. After drinking Schnapps and speculating about all the places on the map, I finally settled on a lake; she immediately and efficiently leafed through railroad maps and timetables and somehow unearthed the telephone number of a hotel by the lake, obtaining the necessary information in a matter of ten minutes.

"It seems nice. I can smell it. I just asked on the phone. It's a middle-sized lake in the highlands, and two years ago a fisherman caught a pike that weighed twenty-eight pounds. But fishermen almost never go there. I asked about the tourists, and he said that there is a camping ground in a nearby forest but that he had only a few guests and that it was very quiet. The campers come to the inn for meals but there are no fishermen there at the moment. I asked about the boat, and the proprietor said that he could lend us one that seats four and that he uses for duck shooting. How does that appeal to you? Does it smell good?"

"I like the part about no one being there."

"It must be full of innocent pike."

"I hope so."

"I'll wear denim pants and a sports shirt. And I'll take one big, fat book. There's no way of telling when I'll find myself immobilized up there while I am with you. I'll have to have something to read. An emergency book, consolation reading, so to speak. I won't feel secure without it."

She went down to the basement and then ran around the room, packing a suitcase. She placed it by the bed so that she could take it with her at a moment's notice, then turned to the wall and fell asleep.

According to her, this place represented a typical modern trend toward providing country simplicity for jaded city folk, and I started to laugh as soon as I saw the inn. There was a remodeled stable connected with the main building by a corridor. This small hotel was situated at the edge of a deep forest. A narrow balcony ran around the second floor, and red geraniums overflowed from the windowboxes, looking like embroidery on the white walls. The pillars, doors, and beams were colossal, thick and heavy, as befit a barn. The only furniture in the small, low-ceilinged room was a bed and a washbasin. The bed was high and, as we clambered onto it, our bodies sank deep into the quilted eiderdown. With a leap, we sank into it endlessly and smoothly as if into the sea, completely buried in crisp, white freshness.

She twisted her body like a cat and laughed: "It's just like a coffin or a cradle."

The road from the inn led into the forest, became a dusky lane that finally ended at the edge of a lake. By walking along the lane farther down, we could grasp the lake's general topography. It seemed to have considerable depth, but its size could be taken in at a glance; as one stood halfway along it and looked to left and right, there were small forests at either ends. On this shore was a forest, a pasture, and a hill; on the other, a hill, a pasture, and a meadow, with a church at the top of the hill. Behind them towered a mountain range. Wide swamps stretched to the water's edge on both shores, and the reeds grew thickly dense and savage, tall enough to hide a standing man. Two streams flowing through the forest lazily emptied into the lake.

"This is it. This is the place," I said. "We'll bring the boat here and anchor it out where it's deep, and cast the line toward the shore. The estuary has made a channel in the reeds. Pike like those shallows in the middle of the channel, on both sides of the estuary around there. You'll be able to catch them."

"You are full of confidence. That's very encouraging. You finally seem to have revived, and that makes me happy. Keep a stiff upper lip. Anyone would think you'd caught something already. That smell you talked about has gone, because it disappears when you get too close. You never know your own odor, do you?"

"Whether you can catch fish or not depends on the mood of the fish. You don't know until you do it, and even after that, you still don't know. In a mountain area like this, there is the wind to consider too. Only the local people know what sort of wind makes for good or bad fishing. Besides, there is an international jinx that says it's bad luck to take a woman fishing."

"That was a long time ago. Now the fish have also changed. The modern fish says: 'Bring women; if you do, I'll be happy to be caught.' Both women and fish are wet creatures; I understand that much. Don't leave me alone tomorrow, all right? I'll follow you all the way. If you can't catch anything, I'll help you with my secret tricks."

As we walked along the forest lane toward the inn, the tree trunks, the bushes, and the road suddenly darkened around us and the rain began to beat down. The forest grew warm and steamy, and the dead leaves, moss, and tree sap all began to smell pungently. And then just as suddenly it began to get chilly. The joyous scents disappeared, trickling back into nooks and corners of the woods. That rain of all rains, the heroic mountain rain, splashed on the leaves and soaked our foreheads and eyebrows.

By the time I ran out of the forest with her, the clouds had covered the sky without our knowledge and had dropped to our eye level like twilight, and the lake surface, which flickered in the corner of my eye, was shrouded by fog. As we ran through the grass, I saw something green flash in a small ditch.

"A frog, a frog!"

I immediately leaped into the ditch and crawled through the grass, covered with mud, trying to capture the slimy, jumping object with both hands.

"A frog, the best! The pike will be happy!"

I pursued it in the deep grass, using my arms to wipe away the rain that spattered my face. Taking care where I put my slippery feet, I grasped to this side and grasped to that, and then suddenly found myself choking. A flood of recollections surged up through my legs and hands. They were so vivid that I felt afraid and suffocated. Had it been twenty or thirty years since I last romped in the rain and grass?

She was watching from the edge of the ditch, and as I finally managed to catch the frog and scrambled up, covered with mud, she curled up with laughter.

"I'm going to get a jar from the innkeeper's wife!" she shouted in a high voice and ran away.

After the evening meal, I went to our room and wound the fur on the artificial fly. Buried in bed clothes up to my waist, I spread all the materials out on the sheet, and engrossed myself in my handiwork with scissors, glue, and thread. I wound various hooks with color combinations of red and white, black and yellow, or red and brown, and attached a spinner to each of them.

"They say that the four basic colors for imitators are red, yellow, black, and white, but red seems especially effective. The red stands out best in the water. One explanation is that it's good because it's the color of small fishes' gills. When large fish chase small fish, the small ones wriggle in their flight, and their gills open and flash red. The big ones remember the color but are also nearsighted; so the moment they see a red flutter, they lose their heads and jump. In other words, red is a delectable color. The fur on this fly opens and closes in water, and the hook is described as 'breathing.' To make it takes skill."

After winding the fur on the hooks, I polished them one by one on an oiled whetstone. I ground them on three sides and finished them with a spear-like tip. Then I pressed the hooks against a fingernail to see if they would bite deeply into the tissue, going in smoothly. The fresh night breeze flooded in from the open window, carrying the invigorating breath of forests, and the mild, thick smell of fertilizer, hay, cattle, and bees. Utterly relaxed, I could concentrate on my fingers. I did not feel myself to be a mass of joined edges of broken pieces, cracks, or holes. Somehow, my internal turbulence had receded far away, and the leaves of my malaise did not thrive, the tendrils sprout, or the roots proliferate. I felt as calm as a lead weight slowly settling in water. Listening to her peaceful breath, I finally felt secure.

We had taken a train that passed through the town at midnight, but I had no idea whether I could make it to the village. I had left the glass house, scraping the countless broken pieces of myself together, barely managing to give them a shape, a knapsack on my back, but I did not know when I would collapse. I didn't know when I would feel the premonition of an avalanche sweeping down my body, or when the ground under my feet would shake and cave in. I went to the station, crept into a berth in the night train, made out a rocky desert on the bumpy iron wall lit by a small reading lamp, smelled the sweet scent of the paint, reached a large junction early in the morning, killed time in the dining room, got on another train, got off at a sunny country station, passed the time on a bench, boarded an old, green mountain train that came late in the afternoon, and was carried slowly along past forests, pastures, and valleys. And all this time, I felt as though I were holding a delicate antique vase part of whose pattern was a mesh of cracks; it was barely held together by adhesive. I felt I had to hold it together as far as the lake. If only I can get to the lake there will be a hotel. There is a room where I can retreat if I collapse. There is a bed. But I don't know what to do if I come apart in a small transfer station in the country.

Sometimes she peered into my face and asked: "Are you all right?"

After a while, she offered me a bag of cherries and asked again: "Are you still all right?"

In the morning, as we were eating steamed sausage and fried potatoes in the dining room of a large junction, she picked up a piece of potato.

"They sell this in London from a wagon and call it fish

and chips. Fried potatoes and small fried fish like sardines or something. When you buy them, they put them in a triangular bag made of newspaper. If you want to take the food home without letting it get cold, you must ask the vendor to wrap it up in a pornographic paper. It will keep nice and warm for a long time. Never, never, even by mistake, let them wrap it in the *Times*; the food will get cold immediately."

She spoke softly, smiling her wry smile, but she looked a little like a college girl, laughing with her mouth full of hamburger.

As we waited for the train on a bench in a little country station, perspiring in the intense white sunlight, or as the diesel engine panted along the edge of a deep valley, she observed my absolute silence and asked from time to time whether I was all right, her apprehension showing in her eyes and on her face. She tried to come over to me but stopped short, and looked at me as though over the edge of a teacup; her voice was as soothing as slow-dripping water. I clearly sensed in her the patience of a woman enduring a painful illness. She was not at all ashamed of her outburst of the previous night, but seemed to be frightened of her own power. I watched her profile as she described how the patterns of the cattle in the pastures which straggled outside the window gradually changed as the train climbed from the plain to the high ground. As she pointed at the cattle in various meadows and put cherries into her mouth one by one, she began to strike me as a bohemian after all, rather than a settled person. She was afraid of herself and yet she resembled a gypsy who refused to be caught by situations and objects. She seemed to be racking her brain to avoid wounding herself and me. I pitied the naïveté of her efforts.

We got up early in the morning, collected a basket packed with lunch from the innkeeper's wife, and at the same time borrowed a tape measure for the fish. I bought a permit at the tackle shop, according to which pike less than forty-five centimeters long had to be put back. Later on, I met the proprietor of the inn. He had a little cabin in the reeds at the lake shore. The cabin is built over the water and the boat is stored under the raised floor. It is moored by an iron chain and a lock. The proprietor offered to let me have the key. He was just entering old age and had a strong body; he looked me over carefully with small, quick, discreet, pale-blue eyes. He was wearing a clean shirt. The small, dark room where he sat was arrayed with a multitude of old tools, a loom, a barrel organ, a blacksmith's bellows, a weather-vane rooster, and other objects. The gigantic head of a pike was displayed on the wall like a trophy, its huge tiger's mouth gaping, baring a mass of sharp teeth. As I looked at this supreme fish, I remembered the old northern saga of a man who lived in a house made out of the ribs of a pike, and I began to think that it was perhaps not total exaggeration.

"It's going to rain all day today. It's supposed to clear from time to time, but I don't know when. I don't fish. I hunt wild duck, since we get good ones in season. So I built this cabin. There is a bed and a lamp, so feel free to use them. I'm delighted to know you are Japanese. This is the first time I have ever seen one, although I heard a lot about them during the war . . ."

The proprietor smiled and stood up, pulling a key chain from his hip pocket—he was broad in the beam, and looked more than a yard wide—and took a key off it.

I turned along the shore and trudged down the swamp road toward the cabin, which was like swimming through deep undergrowth. The morning dew showered from the head-high reeds, and we were drenched in no time, as we shook down the drops from the spiky leaves on their strong stalks.

Suddenly she cried out: *"Hirsch*! Deer, deer! Two of them!"

I stood on tiptoe, in time to see one large and one small deer bounding away. They had probably been grazing nearby and we had surprised them. They did not merely jump, they were pure streaks of light as they cleared the reeds and disappeared into the woods, tawny fire in the dull morning sun.

There was a small pier beside the cabin, and by groping under the bridge I soon found an iron chain. When I gathered it in, an old, scratched, but sturdy aluminum boat bobbed and swayed on the line. I unlocked the chain with the key and towed the boat to the end of the pier, adjusted the oars, and loaded it with fishing gear.

"You know, people around here say the oddest things. This is my first trip to this particular village, but I've been to the region many times before. The people here—couples, lovers, parents, children—all who have close ties call each other turd and rat. It's true. They use these words as if they were 'sweetheart' and 'darling.' My beloved turd, my darling rat! I asked Professor Steinkopf about them and he confirmed that it's a strange but ancient custom. They never use these words when they are visiting a big city, but here they quite openly call each other 'turd' and 'rat,' and I thought I might call you the same."

"What are you going to call me?"

"Instead of your name, I'll call you 'turd.' "

"Add a diminutive to it."

"My sweet little turd!"

"O.K. That's all right."

"Sweet little turd! Sweet little rat!"

"Give me that basket."

"No; call me sweet little rat."

"We're off, sweet little rat."

"I'm going to row, sweet little turd."

She shivered and rose from a crouching position; picking up the basket, she let out an explosive whoop, and ran down to the boat under the dark sky. She sat down quickly in the stern, and grasped the heavy, unwieldy oars; with a push here and there in the shallows she moved skillfully out of the reed-covered inlet into the lake. Mud swirled in the eddies made by each stroke of the oar, but we could see schools of myriad tiny fish swaying like exclamation marks all around us. I was elated at the sense of the lake's fertile wealth.

I fished all morning; when it was almost noon we returned to the duck-hunter's cabin for lunch and stayed there until evening; then we went fishing again. The proprietor of the inn had been right, and the rain poured out of the sky both morning and evening, without letup. The clouds would close in right down to eye level and the rain would bucket down, sobbing in the fog; after a while the clouds would rise and scatter. But soon it would start to drizzle again, and the sky would close in and down would come the rain again. It went on all day long. Mountain rains are cold and severe and pierce you to the bone. The lake only expands with them and provides no shelter. The slightest stir of wind sucks warmth from your drenched body and leaves you freezing. A real downpour causes a shock of excitement in the human body that prevents it from freezing; but a cold, gloomy drizzle traps you in impalpable melancholy and there is nothing to do but tremble and bow your head and bite your lips, feeling as if you were being eaten away. I took off my windbreaker and gave it to her. I had only a shirt on underneath, which was soaked in no time and became waterlogged. The rain invaded every crease of my trousers, socks, and shorts, every dry spot, like a hostile organism and covered my entire body. It even soaked the wrinkles on my asshole. She put on my windbreaker but was no better off than was I. Before long, her hair was drenched and her nose and chin began to drip; she looked as if she had just stepped out of the bathtub. After we returned to the cabin and ate sandwiches for lunch, I made her take off all her clothes and I rubbed her whole body until the skin turned scarlet, then made her drink some Schnapps.

"You'd better stay here this afternoon. It's going to be like this all day. It's not a day for any woman to be outside. I'll go out again in the evening. But you wait here, and read a book or something."

She raised her face, emerging from deep depression. Her hair was plastered on her forehead; her cheeks were blue and her lips had turned purple. Shuddering, she took the small bottle of Schnapps from me and gulped from it, wiping her mouth against the back of her hand. Something like fear or passion flashed in her eyes.

"It's all right. I'll come with you in the evening." She lay down on the simple canvas cot. "Don't worry about me, sweet little turd." She picked up her book.

Each one of us has several, maybe many, different persons within us; the lake is like that, changing constantly.

When I went out again, the water shifted from sparkling to dull, fierce to gentle, harsh to smooth, and still it continued to change. The fields of reeds were sometimes transformed into brilliant patches of golden wheat, or were turned into a desert at the end of the world. The clumps of water lilies sometimes seemed to be growing in a rain forest, and sometimes in an arctic waste. The lake became in turn a gloomy, hidden swamp, or a pool at a tourist resort. I sat in the bow and pointed out which way to go, and she worked the oars obediently, in silence. My mood rose and fell with the caprices of the weather. But this rapport did not last long, for I was worn out, destroyed. Every time the icy water came pouring off my hair and eyebrows and chin, I felt some part of me melt and wash away. The thick fog that accompanied the rain shrouded the lake all around us, and forest, reeds, water lilies, everything faded into invisibility; only the rain and the creaking of the oars remained. There was almost nothing left in me to be touched. Everything was sodden, the starch washed out, the coating peeled off, and what was left would crumble at the slightest pressure of a finger. I was numb, miserable, silent, fretful, and cold, and if anyone had given me a push, I would have collapsed at once in the bottom of the boat like a wad of sodden old paper. A murderous rage started to infiltrate my frozen senses. My body was beginning to shiver, but not from the cold. I felt an urge to pitch out the fishing pole and reel and cling to the edge of the boat with both hands. She did not say a word and continued to row. The sound of the oars made me feel that she was spying on me from behind, following me with slow steps.

Pike lurk in the shade of the shallows. They are killers who glide stealthily from one shadow to another. I try to cast my hook between the leaves of the water lilies. The reel and the pole, fresh from the store, are like artificial arms. I am not familiar with their feel and the hook instantly catches the leaves. I had sharpened it enough to hook into my fingernail, and it bites into anything that it touches. It catches water lily leaves, stems, reed stalks, or rotten roots. The lake is sodden, a viscous, entangled, tenacious thing. It is watching and waiting, spreading its countless tendrils in every direction, and snatching quickly at everything that moves by. You must drop the fly through the narrowest gap between the tendrils and make it seem to swim or flash like a needle through cloth, opening and closing the fur. Each of the lake's tentacles has tendrils of cloudy green scum, which suck in one hook after another. In an empty marmalade jar I had brought the frog I had caught the day before, and I attached a hook to its thigh and threw it in. I took great care, but it snagged immediately on a reed, and I could not recover it even after pulling, shaking, and performing every trick I could think of. All I could do was break the line and go somewhere else.

When it was nearly evening, the lake that had been quiet all day suddenly echoed with noise somewhere in front of us. Twice I heard it, but each time it then receded. I stirred myself and changed the hook in a hurry, exchanging the black-yellow combination for a red-white artificial fly.

"I think they've started to rise. Over there, between those reeds. Would you row us to the deep part? Stop the boat about ten yards away from there. Quietly!"

I glanced back at her as I spoke, and saw that she was so drenched that she could not even raise her head; she was shivering, biting her lower lip. She nodded slightly, bent over the oars, and slowly began to strain with the effort.

The first time I failed. I recovered the hook and cast it a second time. After I wound the reel three or four times and bent the pole in a curve, the line tensed momentarily. An electric shock ran through the pole to my hand, from my hand to my entire body. I jerked suddenly, and the hook probably pierced the fish's lip and bit into the bone. The line began to cut the water and skimmed to left and right.

"It's hooked, hooked, hooked!" I shouted.

"Really!" she cried, half incredulous, and stood up, letting go of the oars. The boat swayed sluggishly. We came back to life. I was revitalized in a second. Instantly my body ceased to dissolve and once again became a tangible entity. All my flesh became firm, I resumed my outward shape, and was dazzled. Sensations pulsed through me, and my body responded with joy. Ruthlessness, irritation, and malice disappeared. I could look at her, not out of the corner of my eyes, but face to face. Her eyes shone, and she quivered all over; she put her hand on my shoulder and burst out:

"I can see it, I can see it. It's running that way, there, it's gone. It's out, it's out again! You've done it, you've done it, my sweet little turd! You did it, didn't you! The little turd won by sheer perseverance!"

She beat her arms, partly in excitement and partly to ward off the cold.

The fish was running through the cold, gray-blue water. It was like a legless crocodile, with white spots on its bright-green skin. Was it eighteen inches long or more? I cautiously pulled in the line and let the fish swim to left and right; when it finally floated to the surface from exhaustion, I drew it slowly to the side of the boat.

"Measure it with the tape."

"Nineteen and a half inches."

"Let it go," I said.

"It's over the minimum size."

"That's all right, let it go."

"We are allowed to take it home."

"Let it go."

Clumsily trying to hold onto the struggling fish, which was spattering noise and water in the bottom of the boat, she raised her bewildered, angry eyes. She seemed genuinely upset.

"We've been rained on all day long, rowed about, lost the hooks, lost the frog, I thought I'd get pneumonia. And after all that, what do you mean let the fish go? Besides, this is over the minimum size and we are allowed to take it home.

The government recognizes your achievement. My little turd, you are shivering!"

"The first one always makes me shiver. I tremble whatever the size. I stake the entire operation on that first catch. That's everything. It's the same with a novelist. It's the initial work that counts. So I'm content. It's all right now. Let the fish go. We were merely playing."

"It's too much for a game!"

"That's why it's so good."

"Isn't it a little late to say things like that?"

She took the hook from the exhausted fish's mouth, letting out a stream of blood.

I took the fish in both hands and put it in the water, and held it until it finally recovered and began to swim on its own. As it regained energy, the fish began to flex its tail slowly. Then I have done enough, I can let go. The pike opened its black, protruding eyes surrounded by golden rings, and after drifting in the water for a while, darted off headlong into the darkness.

She looked at the water absently.

I said to her: "Don't you feel as though you own the lake?"

She turned her angry eyes and retorted: "Such affectation!"

Then she added: "Such complacency!"

After casting several times, I caught the next fish in the same place; it was seventeen inches long and we let it go, too. We moved the boat a little and discovered a narrow channel between a large and a small grove of water lilies, so we tried it and caught a pike thirty-three inches long. It was very heavy and was incomparably stronger than the other two. The line lost its high note, like a violin brushed by the wind; the strength of the fish pulling it down made me watch in astonishment. The thought flashed through my head that the leader might be bitten off by the pike's teeth, and I slid my hand to the brake on the reel. I tightened, loosened, pressed, and relaxed; pulling on the line without a break, I let the fish swim, and, slowly and carefully drew it five inches, ten inches toward me. By the time I had caught this, my third fish, I neither trembled nor felt dazzled. Rather, I tried to enjoy the force of the pull and play with the fish. When it floated to the surface exhausted, turning up its white belly, I tried to get hold of it by putting my fingers into the eyes, but it only slipped away. I borrowed a sodden handkerchief from her, wrapped it around my fist, and thrust my hand into the large mouth with its sharp white teeth. Grasping the lower jaw, I pulled the fish into the boat. A sharp pain ran through my hand despite its protective covering, and as I looked at it, two streaks of blood appeared.

It was not the "pencil pike" I had caught previously. The white belly was heavy with fat and the bright-green skin spotted with white dots was beautiful, but the threatening protuberance of the eyes, the arrogant curl of the lower lip, and the bared fangs were ugliness itself. But there was something that might be called the steely isolation of a male in its prime; it was full of power, and voracious, but somehow an air of resignation surrounded it and I could sense a kind of nobility. As it gaped and closed its gills, writhing and thrashing with great thuds, she became frightened and stood up.

"You've caught a frightful monster."

"No, it's not so bad. When it comes to a fish of this size, each has its own character. This one is beginning to have a sort of personality. Besides, pike are quite delicious, in spite of their ugly faces. The meat is white and firm, there's no smell, and it's good with any sauce. You pack this belly with some fragrant spices and butter and anchovies and bake it. The uglier the face, the better it tastes. The same with human beings. The uglier the couple, the more delicious they are."

"Little turd, you are terrible! You have eaten it and you know all about it, but you gave me all sorts of excuses why I should not. That's what you call selfishness. I'm going to be furious! But let's take this one home and eat it. Tonight we'll poke this monster in the face of the innkeeper's wife. She'll be shocked. And let's drink beer with it, just the two of us, tête-à-tête. Then we can be happy 'absolutely and utterly.' All right? You are looking at a woman who is frozen right through."

"Fine. I'll give you special permission. The small fish will be overjoyed if we kill this one. All the small ones, medium-sized ones, and the ducklings too. It's settled, we'll have this one baked. When the Sakhalin Peninsula belonged to Japan, people used to call this 'yoakashi' [all-night vigil], because they could drink right through the night with such a fish. This one is too much for two. Let's change seats, we've done enough fishing. I'll row this time, little rat."

We had been sitting for hours lashed by the icy rain, and my bones creaked all over when I rose. But it was all right now. I felt confident; I was reborn. Simple, completely fulfilled, and solid.

While I rowed slowly to the opposite shore, the rain stopped and the sky brightened. The water grew smooth and gleamed dazzlingly. The fields of reeds and water lilies and the forests sparkled. The clouds skimmed swiftly over the massive mountain range and the pellucid blue of the sky began to expand, mingling with the red, purple, and gold of evening. I shoved the boat into the reeds on the opposite bank, but the thicket was too dense and widespread for me to move any further. I took off my shoes, stockings, and trousers, and got down into the water. I towed the boat step by step, with the rope from the bow over my shoulder.

"You are very dependable, *little turd*."

"It's nothing, I might as well get even wetter."

"It would be so wonderful if you were like that all the time."

The water reached my thighs; its surface was smooth and tepid, while the bottom was unrelentingly cold. Summer had not yet reached the mud, it seemed. It probably remained just as cold until the fall. I moved forward, groping through the chilly darkness with my toes, avoiding sharp things, spikes and obstructions. The reeds swayed, rustling noisily, and three ducks fluttered up; one huge rat almost as large as a hare swam away; I was transfixed with astonishment at its size. It was as round as a butterball, and as it swam sluggishly away, it turned its head audaciously several times to look at my face. Do field rats behave like that? Or was it a muskrat or something of the sort? I moored the boat to a stump and we crossed a short stretch of swamp. We reached a pasture on the shore. It was a sweeping gentle slope, and in the distance were a church steeple, forests, and massive mountains; there was nothing else except for straggling cattle and trees. As the cattle stood up or kneeled, the bells on their necks clanged, giving off a broad, friendly sound that echoed across the reeds and the lake. The grasses in the meadow were dense, softly lush, and wet, but they soon began to exude the rich scents of evening. She was freezing, so I made her drink some Schnapps and took her under an elm tree. I peeled off her clothes and rubbed her entire body as I had in the cabin. I knew that rubbing with a dry cloth was better; but lacking anything dry, I used my hands. She was ticklish to begin with and wriggled, but when the blood began to glow under her skin she let me do as I wished. At first her body was as cold and heavy as a fruit, but after I had scrubbed her fiercely for some time, it began to relax and go limp. Perhaps because they clung to my body, the scents of dead decaying reeds, of nature, and of the lake itself began to waft around her. The blood came up under her skin slowly, filtering warmly through the white fat. Her body, which until then had seemed like some lost thing under the sky, small and rejected in the deep grass, began to revive as the warm, pink mist spread.

She closed her eyes and whispered softly: "Now, little turd."

She was lying in the cold grass that was darkening in the dusk; her whole head, ears, chin, and cheeks were buried in grass. When I went to mount her, she suddenly looked like a corpse. And I was struck by a feeling that exactly the same thing had happened only recently. It came back to me right away. It was when she first brought me to the glass room where she lived. After sipping some Schnapps, she had mixed bubble bath oil and toilet water in the gigantic bathtub and buried her entire body in the thick, greenish, white foam; only her face still floated above it. I had suddenly associated her face with one lying in a coffin, and the thought must have seeped through to her, for she then told me two lines of her own poem:

The bed in the morning
Is a coffin of marble.

She raised her arms in the grass, smiled, and embraced my shoulders. Only a short while ago, in the icy rain that clung to my body like some fungus, penetrating my flesh to rot my bones, I had felt a murderous impulse. It frightened me but I drew it out, hoping to hold myself together by some sort of passion. It almost made me tremble. Was the flash of murderous anger directed at her? Didn't I feel that she was pursuing me like a hunter? I wanted to concentrate on it, but we were not inside a room where I could really concentrate. The thinking process, which by nature is a secret rite, cannot possibly occur out of doors. Only inside a room can thinking rise up like smoke.

I was replete, free of all complexity and self-disgust. Thoughts could not possibly take shape unless my consciousness was in ferment. No thought, no writing, no words could sprout. My tongue and my fingers did not indulge in their usual tricks. I was as pure and modest as an animal. Cattle were roaming in the meadow and a bell was ringing. I am the cattle, the bell, and the sky. The fresh breeze from the lake comes over the grass and touches my shoulders and stomach; it strokes me with a feather, then circles around behind me and licks every wrinkle of my asshole. My skin is delighted and seems to burn. It is about to burst out laughing, and my backbone almost melts.

She frowned and moaned, grinding her teeth: "There, there! Bump it, it's good. Right in there, push against it."

Suddenly, a fierce, low, scolding groan was drawn from her throat, and she arched backward, carrying me with her. Her chest heaved, her back was bent like a bow, and I was lifted off the grass. All I could do was to cling to her in case I fell. Her white flesh was glowing like a furnace, slippery with perspiration, and I didn't know where to put my hands.

Shortly afterwards, she opened her eyes under my gaze. Even in the now-darkening grass, I could see that her eyes were clear, slightly tinged with blue, and that her climax still resonated in her body.

"Look! An *Abendrot*!"

"Is that German for a red evening sky?"

"Yes. It's famous around here."

"Sun after the rain."

"A mountain *Abendrot*, a real one."

As I looked back over my shoulder, the entire vista stretched before me. Impulsively, I withdrew from her and tried to stand up, but sat back again in the grass. White liquid flowed down my thighs, but I was oblivious. She remained supine in the grass with a quiet smile, and lazily murmured: "This is an unusually beautiful *Abendrot*."

The sky was filled with light. I had seen this in various countries in different parts of the world, but I felt that I was experiencing something completely new, not just an evening glow. Vermilion, deep blue, violet, gold, silver, countless colors had streaked into hazy layers, and while each remained essentially pure, it overlapped with others and flooded the sky. They overlapped and yet did not blur, each remaining absolutely clear, each yielding to the next, each covering another, and creating a crystalline chaos. Night had already invaded lake, forest, and pasture, and, perhaps in response, red and violet had covered the foreground of the sky. In the students' quarters, such light tinted people's faces, clothes, and hands for a brief instant in the evening, and then disappeared. Here the same phenomenon gave a dark shadow and brilliance to every rock, crevice, and fold of the massive mountain, and made the stalk of every reed on the other side of the lake stand out sharply. If a wild duck crossed our path in this brilliance, I could probably see every feather, large and small, and its movement and pause. It was as if some gigantic building were aflame without a wisp of smoke. It was the rise and fall of an empire, without a sound, without a voice, and yet the entire scene was filled with a mighty chorus. While it seemed to move of its own accord, following its set orbit, disregarding its own great song, it was also so fragile that the slight movement of a finger would breach it somewhere.

A tiny glow was visible in the dark forest on the other

shore. It must be the light of the inn. We both stood up, one after the other, and put on the trousers and shirts that were scattered around. They were sodden, and clung to my torso, but somehow I felt no discomfort whatsoever. We stamped on the meadow grass, went down toward the shore, and carefully crossed the swamp, step by step, holding hands, until we came to the field of reeds where the water gleamed stealthily. I untied the rope of the boat. All at once the water, the mud, the lake plants, and the dead reeds began to emit their distinctive nocturnal fragrance, and as I made her get in and pushed the boat into the water, the pike we had thought to be dead jumped with a thud, and gave a deep sigh. It sounded human.

As I coaxed the boat forward, using the roots for leverage, the sharp, dark spikes of reed caught in her hair. When she lifted her face, trying to brush the strands back, her eyes, cheeks, and mouth were tinted purple in the dying light.

"It's been wonderful today, little turd."

"All sorts of things happened."

"I wish this could last."

As I pushed through the field of reeds and came out onto the lake, the red and violet had already faded away, leaving only a residual echoing glow in the west. Demons now appeared at various points on the lake to play their cold-hearted games, applauding each other.

We came down from the mountain.

"Little turd, don't you want to go away? I wish this would last, but I don't think it will; I'm afraid of going home. I'm frightened that it will all revert to the same old thing. So, I'd like to avoid it. Let's go. I haven't seen the city for a long time."

She said this one afternoon about ten days later, while lying under the shade of an elm in the pasture. We had made love deep and long, and now her eyes were dewy and yet clear, with their hint of blue. She had stretched out full length on the soft grass, and spoke softly with a faraway look still in her eyes. Her fear had reappeared somewhere in the distance, and she had already seen it, but she still seemed sure of herself, being able to measure the distance with her eyes.

The next day, we went down the mountain, and after repeating our outward journey, getting on, getting off, traveling, and alighting a number of times, we arrived at "this side of the other side." I had been to this city twice, spending some time there each time. The city's symbol was a black bear, and it had been a magnificent and brilliant capital long ago. It had been totally destroyed in the war, but it had rebuilt itself with invincible energy, and this often made people compare it to Tokyo. But the city had been divided into east and west, and a long, concrete wall stood on the border. While it was no longer a capital, it was a show window of international politics. On both sides of the wall, the inhabitants called the opposite side "over there." Since the nation itself was divided into east and west, when westerners talked about "over there," they meant not only the east side of the wall but also of the entire country. They did not use the name adopted by the new nation in the east, but called it simply "over there." The city existed as an isolated island in eastern territory, and, in addition, was divided in two, within a country that was divided in two. Therefore, when one happened to be in the western part of the country looking eastward and talked about the western side of the city, it was "this side of the other side."

It so happened that I once walked through from east to west immediately after the construction of the wall. I went down the narrow passage carrying a suitcase and stopped at a checkpoint, where a taciturn soldier with hard, sharp eyes examined my passport in minute detail. When it was returned to me and I picked up the suitcase and started to walk, I suddenly realized that I was walking in a white no man's land, and I felt that I had just come out of a vast shadow. The white concrete skin of the road was torn up here and there and weeds had grown through, and the weak winter sun faltered in the absolute stillness. I arrived at the gap in the wall and, as I stepped through, I saw a mass of tourists, buses, binoculars, Kodaks, taxis, and movie cameras jostling one another, but they were just standing there, noisily crowding the place. There was no more white road and I was instantly carried off by a taxi into the ocean of cacophony. The barren white track about a hundred yards long that existed between the shadow and the hysteria came to signify to me the distance between over there and over here, and the wall itself almost disappeared from my memory. As I walked along it, all the encrustations of my life disappeared soundlessly, and I felt as insecure as a naked larva that has just shed its skin, with no prospect of new growth to cover it. But why was it that the fear itself was full of a sweetness that I had never known before? If this is what is called "freedom," I wonder if it is something that only shows its face for a fleeting instant. I wonder if freedom knows no other existence than that of the moment. In spite of the wall, anyone can go from over here to over there. One can ride a tourist bus, or climb up the stairs of the elevated circular railway that runs above the city. One can ride an electric train and get off at the empty station on the eastern side. One will find a checkpoint there and a silent soldier with a hard, sharp face standing in the sentry box. After carefully inspecting one's passport and belongings, he will stamp a twenty-four-hour permit with a big thud. Twenty-four hours later, one will return, and after repeating the same procedure, climb the staircase. The train runs ceaselessly in a circle, day and night, in that side and out this. The subway is managed by "over here," but the elevated railway is operated by "over there." Formerly, it was one of the main arteries of the city; now, probably as a result of the variety of other transportation available, the number of people who use it is extremely limited. Whenever I take it, it's completely empty. Its iron cars are old and creaky and I can almost see the rust on the manually operated doors; but the boxes are sturdy, efficient, and punctual. Although the city is divided into "over there" and "over here," its peerless congenital cleanliness never changes. I have never heard of the government actually ordering the people to clean the city, but there are no flies on either side, and there is no sign of trash on the seats or floor of the train. There are no magazines, newspapers, or refuse lying around; the train is old but clean, thoroughly polished in every corner, and empty. A line of empty iron boxes chained together runs from one empty station to another. They have run uninterruptedly, efficiently, and accurately, day and night, for ten or twenty years, determined never to stop. Anyone can ride in them but no one wants to, and whether there are passengers or not, the trains arrive, depart, and circulate. At the first station, coming from the east, you can look casually up toward its rounded corrugated iron roof and see a soldier with an automatic rifle slung from his shoulder pacing slowly back and forth on a narrow balcony, or just standing there, and you will be informed that this is undoubtedly the farthest "front line."

Kidnapping, wiretapping, disappearances, unnatural deaths in the streets or in hotels, tunnel digging, jumping from windows, spying, defecting, redefecting, pseudo-defecting—

the city's newspapers are full of news of migrations from east to west and, occasionally of movements from west to east and with announcements and interviews comparing things before and after the wall was erected. Even now, odd happenings occur, some involved, some explosive. But the traveler does not encounter such scenes or aspects of city life. Feeling the long wall and the empty trains somewhere in the back of my head, I drift along the wide sidewalk on the main boulevard, cross the white terrace of a café surrounded by red geraniums, and slide past people whose eyes look tired of the summer. They are stuffed to the bursting point with food; they pant for breath, slightly parting thick, wet lips. Their necks are ringed like screw-top bottles with gigantic white rolls of fat that sizzle and melt in the sun. A lethargic youth with piercing eyes sits hunched, hiding behind his somewhat pubic mustache, gloomily angry. On the large, still lake at the edge of the city, boats are floating with billowing red and white sails. Gigantic steel octopus legs can occasionally be seen wheeling through the sky above the amusement park. At various points on the horizon, large concrete boxes tower over the city, which is filled with the brilliance of glass and steel. Watches, perfumes, and furs are displayed in cubes of glass at intervals on the sidewalk, and the random reflections of the gems they enclose scatter exquisitely. Here too, I seem to be a stranger. My premonition is already coming to life.

I decide to sit down in a chair on the sidewalk and drink beer. The well-chilled, strong-flavored, delicate, dense, smooth foam slips down my throat. It is wonderful while I can feel it penetrating my intestines like a mountain stream, but the stream will soon slacken and bloat into lukewarm water, and hot, thick fog will begin to envelop me. And what will happen after that? It is still too far away to tell. I have a premonition but it has not yet taken shape. It is hiding in the cigarette stand, in the geranium bush, and under the grain of the wooden tables with their peeling paint. It is so well hidden that there is not the slightest hint it is there. The sun is catching the grain of the wood and the flow of markings, whose shallow corrugations look like mountain ranges on a map, or the water's edge after the tide has ebbed. The fresh beer streams down into my hot belly, leaving chilly tracks.

"Whenever I come here, I'm always struck by how prosperous it is. The government is frantically trying to seduce people and businesses here by reducing taxes and giving all sorts of subsidies to them. But this city is unpopular except among the oldtimers who miss bygone days, and the population is diminishing all the time. There's no healthy metabolism at work here. The middle-aged people don't settle down because they don't know what will happen next. I often hear it said that this place may die from natural causes. But, whenever I come here, I find it more ostentatious than ever. They spent so much money on the city that I don't think they will let it go easily. And there are other factors, too, besides showing off to the East, I am sure."

She sipped the beer and chattered animatedly, looking over the boulevard with narrowed eyes. Then she suddenly fell silent. She glanced at me out of the corner of her eye and asked me worriedly in a low voice: "Are you all right, little turd?"

I put down the mug and lit a cigarette. The hot flame flickers in the sun. The smoke burns my eyes. Soon, the cigarette stands, the boulevard, and the wood grain of the table will destroy me. The premonition will turn into an abstract disgust, and something that eats through me as slowly as an acid will gradually take shape. I will suddenly feel the ground waver under my feet as I walk down the street.

"... I'm all right for the moment. But I think I'd better

leave after this one because I have an ominous feeling. I'm all right so far—at least I can say that I'll be able to hold myself together for a while yet, until I finish drinking this."

"Do you think you can hold on until we get back to the hotel?"

"I think so, but I may not. I built up my assets at the lake, and I still have some left. But I may go bankrupt all at once. That sort of thing is always happening to me. I'm always piling up toy blocks, one by one, holding my breath, but as soon as I finish what I'm building, it collapses; and then I start building it up again, block by block. It goes on and on repeating itself. I don't get any better or worse no matter how many times I do it."

"You are a strange man, little turd. When it comes to fishing, you stick to it for two or three hours at a time. You survived the experience in the rain at the lake unscathed. And now you can't sit quiet long enough to finish a glass of beer. I wonder what it means. Does it mean that you can't stand cities?"

"That may be it, or then again it may not. I know that I have to do things with my hands and feet, but I don't think that's the whole story, either. Even at my age I still don't know what follows what. I can at least admit that I don't know, which means that I'm now older and wiser to some extent. But the situation hasn't improved one bit. I'm always in a state of inner turmoil."

"It sounds as if we'd better not talk about it."

"I agree."

The hotel had been recommended to us by the information center at the airport. It was a little way off the central boulevard. The ground floor held a camera shop and a dress shop, and as we climbed the dark, sturdy staircase, we found the front desk in a dim corridor on the second floor. A man in late middle age with a dignified forehead like an orchestra conductor's was bending over a newspaper and nibbling at a sandwich like a mouse, alternately taking it out and hiding it behind the counter.

As she took the key from him, she said to me: "You know, if I say to a man like that, 'I'm going to the other side of the wall for a little while; would you be kind enough to look after the luggage while I'm gone?' he will answer, 'With pleasure,' then he will turn aside and mutter something like 'Go to hell.' I'm sure he'll say something. It's happened to me before. Shall I try it?"

The man took the key from the nail, and, as he listened to her, he nodded two or three times. He pointed to the door of the office behind him, returned to his counter, and began to read the newspaper.

She shrugged peevishly and said: "I wonder if he understood Japanese."

The ceiling in the corridor is so high that people unconsciously look up into the stagnating darkness. The door to our room is large and thick, and the ceiling is also high. There is no bathtub or toilet, but there is enough space for gymnastics. Heavy, beige-colored curtains hang at the windows and the floor is covered with a coarse, red carpet; neither is worn nor torn. The walls and the table have no evident stains or scratches, and the slightly aged body of the small reading lamp seems almost cozy. Yet the room oozes desolation. It has something of the air of a warehouse or cattle barn. It feels like something deserted, something no one has entered for years.

The squeals, screams, and groans of sportscars, taxis, and motorcycles flood the room continuously and then fade away. I feel that I am about to be run over at any moment. It is like standing in the street. We close the windows, draw the curtains, turn off the lights, take off all our clothes, and creep under the sheets. The late afternoon stagnates in heat and humidity, but the crisp, white sheets are cool and have sharp edges like mountain water. I sip some Schnapps. Liquid heat with a faint hint of fennel fills my mouth. I move it around a little to soak every corner of my mouth. Then I let it slip down my throat, drop by drop. It has been some time since I last encountered it. I bought the bottle at the airport shop before coming to the hotel. We drank nothing but beer at the inn by the lake, and slowly, while looking at the *Abendrot*; furthermore, we drank only a mugful in the evenings when we returned to the inn exhausted. I didn't avoid Schnapps entirely, but when I tried it once or twice, it tasted like strong acid on my lips, and I gave it up. Yet now I can drink it, taste it, and enjoy it. Obviously, I have changed again.

"Little turd, darling?"

She snuggles down quietly with her cold, pointed nose just tickling my throat and rubs it against my chest.

"It was so wonderful there. I learned a lot of things, and I found out about you. It was a golden summer. Do you remember those deer, the mother and child? They bounded away. It was morning and your trousers were soaked from the hips down by the morning dew, as though you had just come out of the water."

"Of course I remember it, little rat."

I put the Schnapps bottle on the night table and encircling part of the sheet with my arms as if I were playing the children's game of capturing territories, I bury my face in it.

"Do this and you will see the pasture and the cattle."

She chuckles softly, deeply, in the darkness.

I keep my face down and continue: "I can see the deer, and the pike, and the barn."

"Little turd, little turd."

Her hair all disheveled, she laughs, moans, and snuggles

against me, covering my back with her body. As she hugs me and clings to me with strong arms, her breasts are crushed against my shoulder blades and spill around them and her pubic hair presses and scratches against my behind. She bites me slowly, behind my ear, the tip of my shoulder, my neck, and purposefully moves on.

"Ah, little turd, little turd."

Next, she darts her head under my arm and whispers: "My brother."

We got up early every day we were at the lake and returned to the inn late in the evening. We packed a basket with sandwiches made by the innkeeper's wife, and cherries and books, and went to the shore; we pulled out the boat from beneath the duck-hunter's cabin and began to row. Whenever we pushed aside the reeds, which were as strong as bamboo, two deer would invariably spring out from the same spot. According to her mood, she would call them husband and wife, or brothers, or mother and child. We always rowed out first to the deep water, and then slowly and stealthily came back to shore and cast the line, aiming at the thicket of reeds or under the water-lily leaves. Every day, the first catch was all-important. After the second one, I took my time and enjoyed watching them writhe, struggle, and sway; I liked to see the fresh green-and-white-spotted bodies flash and swim in the smooth water. No matter how many I caught, I let them all go regardless of size. By the time they left my hands and their tails disappeared into darkness, the tyrants that glared at me with gigantic protruding eyes had come to look as meek as puppies.

Sometimes we returned to the inn for a nap, and then started out again in the evening; other times we stayed at the lake all day. In the morning, the water grew warm as the sun rose, and dipping a foot in it felt like being licked by a dog.

(157

On days like that, we rowed the boat across the lake and landed on the opposite shore. She carried the basket on her arm and I slung a water canteen over my shoulder, and we walked from meadow to meadow, from hill to hill. As I worked the big oars to move the boat from one place to another, or marched ahead of her panting, steeped in the scent of grass and perspiration, I felt as though alcohol and nicotine were being squeezed out of the very marrow of my bones. From my hands and feet, shoulders, hips and knees, from each part of me that ached and poured sweat, a thick, viscous poison of accumulated monologues and soul-searching oozed out of my skin, and then both perspiration and poison vanished, swept away by the breeze. We grew fit and clear-skinned, lit up by the sun that penetrated into our very innards. We forgot about criticizing each other and being criticized, and no longer felt depressed or downcast. There were a number of sheds in the meadows to shelter the cattle from showers and rain. These had no doors; they contained nothing but hay and, as we became physically conscious of each other in the overtones of our lively banter and in our glances, we unhesitatingly entered one of the sheds. We stuck a fishingpole in the mud at the entrance, tied a handkerchief at the top, and made love in the hay. The hay had an honest, sweet smell that was somehow also rather heavy. We gazed unashamedly at odd parts of our bodies and explored them with our tongues, and when a piece or two of hay got tangled in hair and we bit into it, all we had to do was to giggle and blow it away.

Sometimes I said: "There, on the other side of my chin," or, "Yes, all the way along the ridge," or "Try biting the wrinkles, lightly."

We slept in the downy, luxurious hay; the scent was powerful, and the sun continued to stream in through gaps in the wall or the knotholes in the planks, although it sometimes grew so bright that it woke us. It touched the thin skin of my eyelids, and mingled with memories of her moans and my surging ejaculation, which had been like waves breaking through my penis; I floated while I slept. It felt rather like sliding down a stream under the red glow of the sun, floating half submerged, buoyed by the water, rather than sinking into sleep in a cool shade.

When I open my eyes, the sun has moved considerably; sometimes she is dozing beside me with her mouth slightly open, sometimes she is reading a book and looking serious, and at other times she may be sitting in the grass, making a chain with fragile flowers picked in the meadow. I open my eyes and go to stand at the entrance of the shed, looking out over the lake, the field of reeds, the village, the pastures beyond, and the delicate clouds drifting above all, tinted with the red of evening; suddenly she will appear from the meadow and hand me a bouquet or a garland.

"This looks like a chrysanthemum, doesn't it?"

"Isn't it wild camomile?"

"Little turd knows everything."

"They are all wild guesses, little rat."

"Don't be so modest."

She moves majestically, stamping on the grass, showing off her broad shoulders and strong hips, but when she walks off with her back toward me, or crouches in the grass looking for flowers, there is something forlorn about her, although she is neither frightened nor lonely. As I look at her, I am reminded of the sight of her completely surrounded in her spiritual isolation by the first-class merchandise spread all over the floor of the luxurious glass room, of her laughter and shouts of "never underestimate a woman!" and of her alienation because she was unable to leave so much as the mark of her fingerprints on them. Just as she was alienated from the sealskin coat, keeping it fresh yet not possessing it, she now seems to be isolated from and rejected by the camomile flowers. No matter how much she stomps over the meadows, not a footprint of hers will remain. This isolation is at the root of the forlornness I see in her.

"Now, little turd, pull yourself together!"

She kneels down on the grass, lightly touches my trousers with her fingers, and pulls down the zipper; the object that had been dormant until this moment, rises as soon as it feels the touch of her slim fingers. She closes her eyes and takes it into her mouth, and then lets it go with a popping sound and hangs the clover nosegay over it. She bends over, shouts with laughter and applauds wildly, then jumps about. In the first dusk, still tinged with red, her voice peals out through the fog that rises from the lake, through the sound of bells on the necks of distant cattle, and through the rustling of tiny secret little creatures and its clear notes travel an amazing distance.

The loud, hoarse, but strident noise of a sports car suddenly tears through the room. Everything, including the windows, shudders, then recomposes itself, and quiets down. I pull her head up gently from her task, the meticulous and minute pecking of a little bird buried in the depths of the sheet. She slowly comes up, rubbing against my hip, side, and chest.

She mumbles in a muffled voice: "You caught a lot of pike. I didn't know that such fish existed. I've been living here for ten years and still didn't know about them. The hotel proprietress stuffed it with spices and baked it, and I never dreamed it could be so delicious. It made me think. The oldtimers in the village were full of praise for you; they said you were a true fisherman and a real man. They show up at the same place at the same time every night to have a drink. Every night without fail. And they all have their regular places. When you presented them with a large fish you made them very happy. It was a very nice thing to do."

"They say no two lakes are the same. Even one lake is constantly changing. It takes time to appreciate this and to learn the right way to cast a bucktail fly. That lake has its own idiosyncrasies. Pike jump at anything and everything, but when they don't want to bite, they don't bite and no master angler can do a thing about it. It was neither spring nor fall but summer when I caught the fish. You must give me credit for that. The fishing saved me. It gave me a little confidence."

"I watched her in the kitchen and learned a good deal. White sauce is difficult to make and I must study it more, but I think the trick is to put anchovies in it. The saltiness complements the white meat of the pike. I'll cook it for you next time. You can survive in the wilderness for a long, long time if you take me and one frying pan along with you, little turd."

"That's good! Shall we do it again and finish our summer project? Tomorrow, you can look around the fishing tackle shops here and gather some information. We'll glean as much as possible, pool our facts, and analyze them; then I'll tell you which is the best place to catch fish. It's very exciting to look for a secret fishing place on the map of a part of the country I've never visited before. You can be the scout who just reports back to me. I'm the chief of staff."

"All right. Leave it to me. It makes me happy to hear you talk like this. It will be so wonderful if you are like this all the time. It's hard for me to watch you collapse. It makes me follow suit. I'm strong, but I collapse if I'm attacked at one particular point. I do have such a weak spot. And you start digging at it ruthlessly while you yourself are flat out on the bed. That's how things like the other day happen. You never relent, do you? You hide it in front of other people, but you couldn't help being ruthless even if you tried. And you blame yourself afterwards, you turn the edge of your criticism on yourself as well as on others and you suffer it twice over. That's why you are cruel. You cannot love anyone, you cannot stake your life either, because you can't forget yourself. Or so it seems to me."

"I can't forget myself, so I can't escape myself either. Whether I go out or look inward, it's the same. There's no escape."

"This is becoming a strange conversation for a bedroom scene."

"But what you said was true."

"Was I right?"

"Not completely, but you were fairly accurate."

"I don't like it."

Suddenly her soft hair fell over my face as a motorcycle roared outside. Her lips moved passionately, devouring everything, leaving their mark on skin that has been sensitized like thin tissue. They glided all over, trembling, casually stopping to linger, or suddenly jumping in an unexpected direction. All these individual impressions fused into one, and soon a kind of gloomy desire overtook us. Every time her hair veiled my forehead and nose, I remembered her chuckling in the cowshed and throwing showers of hay over me.

There seem to be no organs that are as constantly exposed to the light and as ceaselessly abused as human lips. They scarcely ever remind me of their presence, nor are they conscious of themselves. But when they are kissed for two or three hours on end, there are moments when everything suddenly melts. I don't know when they come, or from where. The weight of each separate body disappears. Unsightly bones, heavy flesh, unwieldy fat, everything flows in a single molten stream in the late hours of the hot, overripe summer afternoon. Every part of us is hot, deep, and wet. Something

(162

spreading and vague like mud or honey radiates incandescent white light and an inner darkness like a furnace, and floats up from a wrinkled, crumpled bedsheet with a cry. Gentle chaos spreads everywhere. Lips, teeth, face, everything dissolves, leaving me conscious of just one tiny point on the tip of my tongue, and then the chaos spreads outward from that point in front of my eyes, but not behind. Two sea lions play in a bright sea, floating and diving. The water of the autumn lake laps the feet of the pier. Idling on the drifting white flesh of a jellyfish, I gaze into infinity as revealed by this chance game.

She raises her hand sluggishly and wipes her tears in silence. By the third hour of love-making, it is only the anus that refuses to relax. It is tightly clenched, with a collection of little wrinkles. But even that is buried too deep. The fragrance of toilet water spreads luxuriantly and wafts through the room, mingling with her scent, and sweat films from our bodies. As I penetrate her through this film, there is no customary quiver in the right or left wall where I usually find it after the greeting kiss, but only the sensation of a fetid swamp. She does not respond, though I reach the point where I usually wait, play a little, and touch the inner wall. Could it be that her flesh has ripened completely and dissolved? Every fiber, sinew, and kernel seems to have been broken down by the all-engulfing heat. I slide into the hot stream and slowly, in a daze, sway back and forth in the curtain of mist. Suddenly, for no reason at all, the moment of fear overtakes me without a hint of premonition. The chaos darkens and fades. I am pushed upward, and yet my shoulders are thrust down by something and I crumble. I feel my backbone tremble and my abdomen catch on fire, and I sense that shapes full of savage turbulence are already looming in various corners of the darkness. I collapse.

Somewhere, a vague voice murmurs.

But it did not last.

Almost every morning, she is in the habit of looking at her arm the minute she opens her eyes. She stretches it out from the sheet and inspects it thoroughly, turning it this way and that in the dim, shadowy light. She did so in her glass room and also in the country inn. After gazing at it in silence, she mutters to herself: "Yes, it's all right," or laments that she has grown old. Sometimes, she extends it toward me, saying: "Would you please look at it, how do you like it?" Some mornings it certainly deserves to be called a masterpiece. Under the delicate skin that absorbs rather than repels the probing finger and holds it there, there is a layer of exquisite flesh and cold fat. No hair, freckles, blemishes, or pores. The blood lies deep and everything is clear and blue. Yet this layer is heavy with the clear, pale trace of deeply hidden veins. It is impressive enough to inspire one to confidence all day long.

"Even the porcelain vases of the Yi and Ming dynasties aren't as good as this," she said again this morning. "I compared my arms to them at the museum some time ago. There were pieces of Ming, Sung, and Yi, but they did not compare with my arm. It's a shame that it's all I have to show at my age. But it still commands a price. It's what the Chinese used to call 'the cold clarity of unctuous jade.' "

She laughed and left the bed after scrutinizing her arm in the bright sun that streamed through a gap in the leaf-brown curtains. I was dozing contentedly, hugging the crumpled pillow under my chest, as if it were filled with fresh milk. Noises were already rising from the streets, and the light that fell on my eyelids was refreshing but already bore signs of mild heat.

"There is something big in the paper, little turd," she said in a muffled voice, holding a newspaper in one hand while brushing her teeth with the other. She slowly paced the room as she read the news aloud.

". . . as a result of signs that have been noted for the past three or four weeks, there is rising speculation that the major communist offensive on Saigon will take place in the near future. The communists had called for a total uprising of the people of Vietnam to coincide with the Tet this year, and also mounted attacks on various cities in May. They were forced to retreat but now they seem to be planning a third offensive. The South Vietnamese government has issued a warning to both army and civilian personnel and the curfew has been advanced by an hour. A high-ranking officer at the U.S. Army headquarters said: 'We won't be surprised if they come. Anything can happen here, and we are well prepared. Let the commies come and we'll smash 'em.' Does he mean the reds when he says 'commies'?"

"Right."

"They sound as if they are in high spirits."

"What press service is that?"

"WAP."

"What else does it say?"

'That's all. Nothing else. Are they really going to attack? That's wonderful! Do you think this is going to be the show-down? You can't lie around, little turd. But it may be only a rumor, because I can't smell anything. I can usually sense when something's cooking."

"I don't know. Over there, there is fierce fighting every spring and fall. It has to do with the rainy season and the harvest. It's a question of securing either rice or manpower.

Actually it can happen at any time, not just in spring and fall. 'Anything can happen,' is right. That statement in itself is accurate."

"The same thing is true here."

She brought the newspaper over, put it quietly by the pillow, and went to the washbasin to clean her face. I got out of bed and picked up the newspaper, but I didn't know which column had the news. I finally managed to decipher the printed letters "Saigon." It was not a long column. It occupied about as much space as there would be for an earthquake in a distant country or the kidnapping of a foreign ambassador. It was only natural that she couldn't smell it.

"I'm going out for a while now. You need shaving cream and a razor, and tissues, right? After I go around and gather information from the fishing tackle shops, I'll buy a map. We'll have lunch together. You can analyze the fishing spots, drink beer, and find a secret fishing place; is that settled?"

She waved her hand, saying "goodbye now," and went out of the room. Before I was aware of it, she had become a housewife and donned her shell, just the way a clam does. She had an air of solidity and assurance around the shoulders and hips. She was vivacious and confident; her eyes and face looked serene, open, and content. I had asked her to make our affair no more important than children playing house, but my request had had as little effect as a baby's nonsense talk. Suddenly I felt an upsurge of nameless depression, accompanied by a vague irritation. She finally seemed to have discovered the domestic life which I had known at the age of eighteen. She was pathetically lively and overexcited.

After she left, I smoked a cigarette, lolling in the hollow of the mattress. I could feel the aftereffects of this great shock all over me as if I'd been delivered a dull blow. It was as if I had glimpsed something entirely foreign to me, or had been slapped across the face. Suddenly a faceless beast appeared; it didn't attack me, didn't even pay any attention to me, but sprawled insolently on the floor. It had suddenly emerged, after tiptoeing up on me, from behind the man with the frog, the glass room, the squirrel, her tears, the rainswept lake, and her dissolving vagina; whenever I had glimpsed it before, it had always been with its back to me, which had left me off guard. I was distraught; I didn't know whether what I could see was only a part of it or the whole. I listened to the noise outside the window and pressed my nose against the sheet, which had soaked up our fluids from the night before. As I watched the sun dancing on the ceiling and the wall, I began to swell, although rooted to the spot. I became shapeless, and began to suffocate. The root began its irrevocable growth, leaves burgeoned, and vines seized me in their tangles. I felt as if I must crumble to nothing if I didn't move. The new strength I had managed to build up so fast at the lake was almost exhausted. My usual affliction had started in the stifling heat.

I wrote a note that she would find when she returned, put it in the middle of the table, and left the room to go to the station. It was easy enough to find it and then an information booth. I asked whether there was a branch office of the press service in the city, and after being given the address and telephone number on a piece of paper, I showed it to a taxi driver. The office occupied three dark rooms of an old building just off one of the boulevards: in it a number of men and women were smoking or banging away at typewriters. A telex whined and rattled, spitting out papers that spread in serpentine folds over the linoleum floor. I spoke to a large man near the entrance and showed him the identification cards I had used three years ago as a temporary roving reporter for the press service, my U.S. field permit, and all the other cards that

I had always preserved as mementos. I gave him the names of a reporter and a cameraman who had worked for their particular press service's Saigon branch in those days. At first he seemed puzzled and hostile, but when he heard the names, he smiled. We chatted a little about the reporter in question—his nickname and idiosyncrasies. He brought out two or three files and put them on the table. Pulling up a chair, he told me to sit down and to read as much of them as I liked.

"Are you a reporter?"

"No, I'm a novelist. I sometimes work as a reporter, but I'm usually involved in a novel. I'm on vacation now, but I happened to read your wire story this morning."

"Are you going to write an article?"

"No, it's just for my personal interest."

The big man seemed to be satisfied, and went off to another seat, leaving a strong reek of body odor; he leaned against the chair, and began to chatter lazily with his colleague.

I left the office late in the afternoon. I had spent almost a half day there, but the information I had gleaned was minimal. I read the files, but I did not feel that I could penetrate what might have been behind those news items. I had limited the articles in the files that I read to those of the last six months, but they were filled with records of countless battles, or rather, mere names and numbers, and the connecting thread was not easy to find. On the other hand, the political data that cropped up here and there in the statements and comments of high officials gave me few clues as to their origin; I could not tell whether they had emerged from bloodshed on the battlefield, whether they signified a major trend, or were merely coincidental. I thumbed forward and backward through the mass of papers, sometimes riffling the pages, at other times just sitting in a stupor.

Occasionally, when I came across the names of small towns where I had stayed, or even spent the night, the thick fog that erased all faces from my memory lifted; a clear picture would suddenly flash between my eyes and the page, although I believed I had long ago destroyed my real recollection of such things by reminiscing about them too often. These flashes were constantly changing and superimposing themselves, one upon another, until they probably retained none of my original impressions; I must have been looking at scenes from my own private country of the mind, so to speak. At any rate, I saw them for a second, quite vividly: the wide, slow-flowing yellow river, floating water hyacinth groves as large as islands, lizards crawling on the damp, crumbling lamp-lit wall, and a dead soldier's dog, which followed us tirelessly during our retreat through the jungle, where the evening light seeped in like water.

When I returned to our room, she leaped from the bed and scolded me: "Where have you been? I was worried to death, even though you left a note. A sick man shouldn't wander around alone so much. You ran away the minute I turned my back. I can't be too careful with you, turd." She was angry.

After taking a shower, I lay down in bed but I could not sleep. I lit a cigarette and put it out, and then another, and another, until finally evening came. She said that she wanted to talk about the lake in peace and quiet, and laid the table with all the food she had bought for dinner. A roast chicken, ham, Gorgonzola cheese, dill pickles, pimentos, olives, cherries, red wine. She skillfully carved the chicken, using only a pocket knife, and laid the table with pieces of newspaper in place of plates. The morning paper with its news column was immediately covered in grease and sauce, and was discarded an hour later in the wastepaper basket. The wrappings for the ham and cheese were also thrown out. The chicken became a bunch of bones and was also discarded, wrapped into rather a large ball.

"Chicken or duck, the skin is the best bit. And the other good part is the meat around the thighs, or the pope's nose. That's tasty. You should try it, and you'll see what I mean."

As I talked, I could feel that all-too-familiar vacuum expanding in the smooth, rich aura of the wine. The emptiness of what I said, the emptiness behind my brain slowly began to take over.

Sipping the wine slowly, she spread the map on the table. She laid out her notebook and gave me the detailed information she had collected from every fishing tackle shop she had visited that day. This front-line city had everything, and seemed to have fishing tackle shops too. On a piece of paper she wrote down all the names of the lakes that had been mentioned to her, looked for them on the map, and she marked them one by one. Holding a red pencil in one hand as she pored over the map, she seemed solidly happy again, excited and free from shadowy ghosts.

"You said that it's better to have a lake that's fed by rivers than one that's landlocked. The more tributaries, the better, and the rivers should be flowing out as well as flowing in. The best thing is a group of large and small lakes connected by rivers. In other words, each one is an open lake that is connected to all the others; isn't that what you said was best? You called it a system, or something. You've taught me something new. The place in this area that's made to order is in the eastern sector. In the west, we'll have to go far. First we have to get out of here by airplane and go to some large town; after that we'll find it."

"We'll think about it tonight. You don't have to hurry. The closer it is to autumn, the more greedy the pike get. So, the later, the better. This is something we can take our time over. The more you wait, the better it will be. But the other thing is not the same. There's something suspicious about it. It's beginning to smell."

"Let me hear about it; tell me!"

"It's a story about politics. It's about war, so it has to be about politics. In other words, it's both rock-hard and as slippery as an eel and I can't quite put my finger on it. They say that if you don't want to lose friends, don't talk about politics. It's good advice. Do you think it's all right to talk about it? Don't you think it might spoil our relationship? I've had bad experiences in the past. I can almost bet something will go wrong."

"It's all right. I'm prepared."

"Are you sure?"

"I'm ready, tell me."

"Someone has said that discussing politics in a novel is like listening to music at a concert and having someone fire a gun in your ear. Who was it? Stendhal? It doesn't matter. It's another piece of good advice. It's an aphorism by someone who knows his way around."

"It's all right. It's the times and I don't think you can avoid talking about politics. Besides, there are concerts and concerts. Take a concert of *musique concrète*. A shot in your ear would be an anticlimax. This is the era for that sort of thing. I think it would be better than having you sulk in a corner of the room. Having you sulk when I know why is better than getting irritated without knowing a thing. Tell me."

"I think you'll be sorry."

"It's all right. Tell me."

I put out the light, leaving only the reading light on, and she climbed into bed and cuddled against me, holding a wine glass in one hand. I propped up my hot, heavy body and lit a cigarette. My arm and torso could feel her soft, strong body quietly breathing, and her pervading fresh warmth. The window turned red and then blue, and the sound of an engine or the squeal of tires pierced the darkness from time to time. I felt only vaguely cruel and was conscious of my belly, heavy and warm with wine; I did not know how to channel the flood of my emotion.

They used a lunar calendar over there, in which the New Year fell in February. Because of their position in the monsoon belt, their New Year was hot and humid. The people were poor but on this day they dressed up, ate sumptuous dinners, visited their relatives and friends, and the children ran around lighting firecrackers, which often were mistaken for gunshots. The flower vendors brought in myriads of flowers from the countryside to sell. In addition to tropical flowers such as hybiscus and bougainvillaea, temperate flowers such as chrysanthemums, narcissus, peach and plum blossoms, and roses were sold. It was their custom that battles be limited to forty-eight or seventy-two hours. It was also customary that each side declared an armistice of its own and took a rest. This year, the antigovernment forces began an armistice on January 27, followed by the government forces' armistice on January 29. Then, on January 30, the antigovernment troops suddenly launched a total offensive and invaded Da Nang, Hoi An, Kontum, and Nha Trang, provincial capitals and military bases or installations, causing much destruction and damage. The next day, the thirty-first, the whole remaining area including Saigon and Hue came under attack. In Saigon, a special task force of nineteen members attacked the American Embassy; after they had destroyed most of it, all nineteen were shot to death. There was heavy street fighting throughout the city. It lasted for twenty-four days in Hue. It was reported that, out of the total population of forty-five thousand, thirty thousand were made refugees. It was estimated that the offensive forces numbered approximately six thousand. It was reported that the National Liberation Front's Fourth, Fifth, and Sixth Commando Units made up the nucleus of these forces. During the twenty-four days of fighting, the antigovernment forces declared the establishment of a provisional government, appointed a university professor as the governor of the province, and held a people's court. It was reported that several thousand antigovernment forces, several hundred American soldiers, several hundred government soldiers, and approximately twenty-five hundred civilians were killed. However, these several thousand could become several hundred, and vice versa. Or it might be better to quote no figures at all and simply state that the civilians were killed as they fled, the American soldiers in battle, the antigovernment forces in revolutionary struggle, and the government soldiers in wholesale rout, plunder, rape, and aggression.

". . . This is what happened in February, the so-called Tet offensive. And then in May, they carried out a general offensive on a smaller scale all over the country and then retreated. They advanced and withdrew in February, and then advanced and withdrew again in May. There was an interval of three months between the two. It may mean that the reorganization of their forces took three months. And that in turn means that the third offensive will be in August. The government will prepare for it, so they may delay for another month and attack in September. Every autumn, they organize a fall offensive and the fighting becomes ferocious; judging by that, I think it's better to say that we can be certain of a third wave sometime between August and November. In addition to the questions of rainy season, dry season, or harvest time, Hanoi and the National Liberation Front celebrate a number of commemorative days during this period. One should look out for them. And Saturday nights—if a moonless Saturday night and a commemorative day coincide, it smells for sure. Even if they don't fall on the same day, if they occur close enough to each other, there's a possibility. I tried to check on them today, but there was none of the necessary data.

"On the other hand, there's another factor. The Tet offensive was in February, and the partial bombing halt in the north was in March; the second wave was in May and the peace talks were started on May thirteenth. I don't know at all what sort of contacts were made at the top level on both sides, but the war seems to have a physiological make-up that produces fierce battles when there is a possibility of peace negotiations. It is an old adage that when people start talking peace, they can expect a great and sudden disaster. Dien Bien Phu happened in the midst of the Geneva Conference. Negotiations on the one hand and fighting on the other. If you want to stop a dispute, there's nothing to do but fight. If this sounds too easy, you could say that in order to stop some people spitting saliva, you must spill other people's blood.

"So far I've given you a digest that I picked up from papers in Tokyo; it's an outline that everyone knows. But, when I was checking today, I found out that General Vo Nguyen Giap had advocated a quick, brutal showdown, which turned out to be the Tet offensive. Why? They don't know his motivations. But there is something called 'the ninth decision.' Its official title was the 'Vietnam Labor Party Administration's Ninth Decision,' issued by the Central Committee of Hanoi, and was probably transmitted to the southern jungles and villages. In other words, it was a command decision from the highest level. This ninth decision appeared after the Tet offensive and is said to have ruled that a massive attack by large battalions had been a mistake from the strategic point of view.

It presumably ordered the troops to revert to guerrilla tactics. In other words, the Tet offensive was a failure. This may be the reason that the second wave in May was smaller. From the very beginning, Hanoi's intention was to draw out the war and to nibble off territories little by little by guerrilla warfare and local battles, forcing the Americans into a demoralizing bout of shadow boxing. After a while, the Americans, frightened by the shadows that can be cast by mounds of corpses, would react in disgust and also suffer an economic slump. Then the antiwar faction would gain ground and the country would be polarized. In other words, they intended to cause a large hemorrhage by bleeding a little here and a little there, instead of piercing the heart. They had no choice but to fight that sort of battle and they did exactly that. I knew it and I always thought they were succeeding. So I couldn't understand why they came out with the Tet offensive. Even with the news of General Giap's quick showdown theory, I still don't understand his motivation. If Hanoi judged it to be a mistake, it means that both sides in a war make mistakes. It seems only natural, but you often forget that they both do."

"Does that mean that thousands of people were suddenly killed in the midst of the New Year's celebration and tens of thousands of people became homeless because of General Giap's mistake?"

"If you forget that it resulted in the partial bombing halt in the North, and in the well-learned lesson on the part of the Americans that they couldn't possibly defend the territory, and in the fact that it exposed the Saigon government, both officials and soldiers, to the eyes of the world as nothing more than rotten men of straw, if you exclude these things, it means exactly that. However, my impression is that Hanoi's mistake was their misjudgment that if they attacked, the people of the South would welcome them and rise up in arms; in reality, it didn't turn out that way. When they thought up their slogan of total war, they probably included the entire populace in addition to the whole army. In Hue, a small segment of students and civilians seems to have armed and joined them, but they were of minimal significance. At any rate, the population as a whole did not rise, and yet, contrary to the analysis of the Council's ninth decision, they still seem to be advocating total insurrection over the entire country. This has, of course, been a slogan from the very beginning, and I can't quite see the difference."

"Your talk is all *seems* and *maybe's*. It's odd that when you try to be accurate, you only become vague. Is it because you are guarding against judgments based only on information available in the West? My impression is that this whole affair sounds terribly important and yet it couldn't be more vague."

"It's because this is all I could get out of the files. I went through the papers and print-outs with a fine-tooth comb. I can't do any more than that. I can make conjectures but I can't say anything definite, since I haven't seen it with my own eyes. Even if I had, it would be difficult to arrive at the truth."

"Then can I say that all your talk is mere humbug? If you can't say anything decisive, then perhaps I am free to do so. May I repeat that all your talk is nonsense? I think it's permissible."

"What is it that you are saying?"

"I have a hunch. But I don't know for sure. I'll tell you when I've confirmed it. I don't think I'm wrong but I'm not sure. Give me a little more detail concerning what you found out. How did the special task force slip into Saigon?"

"Infiltration in itself is nothing. It's the same as asking how water can pass through a sieve. They are right there from the beginning and even if they did come from outside, it was still easy. They must all have special permits to enter, but such papers are easily forged. They came in droves by taxi, ferry, tricycle, and bus. They carried machine guns in coffins. Rockets were transported by florists' trucks under flowers. The sentries have radar but all you have to do is to give them two or three coins. Actually you don't even have to bribe them; one glare will do the job. Speaking of the special task force, they were quite ordinary looking. They were wearing white shirts buttoned up to the neck, and those wearing the peasant's uniform of black pajamas had red armbands. And there must have been many other devices known only to them. But I would have to qualify this statement too."

"In brief, when the civilians were relaxed and happy, sleeping off the New Year, they attacked by the front door, hiding behind flowers? It's cowardly. Is it all right for the people's army to do that kind of thing?"

"How about the wooden horse of Troy?"

"But . . ."

"Washington, too, crossed the river and attacked the British army, while the British were celebrating Christmas. It's the same kind of thing. The people's army is military too. The people's war is also a war. It's neither new nor exceptional in any way. Since we are dealing with war and an army, no matter how they advocate good behavior as their motto, it must be within the requirements of over-all strategy, and good behavior must meet their needs. Once it diverges from military strategy, it must be ruthlessly checked. There's no room for hesitation. The people's army, too, must kill people, both before and after the revolution. 'Maybe,' that is, of course."

"It couldn't be helped if the special task force members who attacked the American Embassy were all killed, and they were probably prepared for it. But if the general public was involved, how can you justify it? The end justifies the means and the means are formulated and regulated by the end, they say. The end probably means the political effects. But I wonder how they can win the support of the people by such an action. It probably did effectively demonstrate to the people that the whole thing hinged on the presence of the Americans, but how can you explain it if the people felt that both sides behaved with equal atrocity, Americans and Vietcong? What are you going to say to that?"

"There's only the one or the other over there; they are either progovernment or antigovernment; that means kill or be killed. So if you look at the result, silence is hardly the third choice, is it? If you keep silent, it may mean that you don't care who wins, but, in effect, it means that you are supporting one or the other. Neither side would particularly like to have the people silent; but if you ask yourself which side is more corrupt, there is no question about it at all. As it is, an army sent overseas has no roots and is inevitably demoralized. The National Liberation Front scattered leaflets among the camps of the government forces and appealed to the soldiers saying, 'We don't want to kill you, help us if you can; if not, hide somewhere and do not interfere.' Silence means participation, complicity."

"Do they mean it? Or is this another war tactic?"

"Depends on the situation; it could be either."

"You've made a judgment."

"No, I haven't yet."

"Yes, you have."

"I'm just talking."

"You said it depends on the situation."

"I said, 'without looking at the situation,' right?"

Suddenly she drew back. It felt as if something had been peeled away from my stomach and arms. I was unburdened and a hole appeared in the sheets. Turning over, I saw her broad hips and white buttocks rising in the dim light; she disappeared into the darkness with slow steps. Somewhere there was a faint metallic squeak; a fresh breeze flooded into the room along with the outside noise and streaks of sun fell here and there. But the rustling forest creature that sprang to life inside me the moment she drew back swelled to occupy the whole room; not even the breeze could dispel it. She crossed back slowly, holding a wine jug in her hand, and stood beside me; she poured some wine in the empty glass.

"You intend to go back there, don't you? One reason is to escape from me, isn't it? You were really aroused."

She spoke these words quietly, but with a piercing sharpness. The light just reached her breasts and I could vaguely see her torso, her navel, and her pubic hair through the pink silk haze, as well as her hand clutching the neck of the wine jug. I was shattered by her animal intuition. I was afraid to stretch or look up at her eyes in the darkness. I didn't have the courage to protest that she had misunderstood me. She was mercilessly, perfectly accurate. While I went rambling on inanely, she had probably been ahead of me, lying in ambush, holding her breath. When I finally showed a momentary hesitation, she had reached out her hand and pushed me over at a touch. That was enough. Embarrassment spread through me like mud and oozed out of my pores.

"Tell me about three years ago. You never tried it, so I never asked you. How was it in the jungle? I don't mean the opium den. You must tell me that first. I just want to ask, that's all, you don't have to worry. I shouldn't have been so shy about it, if it was all going to end like this."

She slowly came around the bed and slipped in between the sheets, shoulder first, but she agilely avoided my body.

(179

Noiselessly, she fitted herself back into the hollow she had made before and did not move an inch.

She had the eyes of a whore.

Once more, I begin to make artificial flies.

I start to read the newspapers every morning. I wake up, wash my face, go out to eat at a nearby café, buy as many newspapers and weekly magazines as I can understand, and read the international columns. I ask her to translate this country's newspapers, which I cannot read. Over there, trivial battles seem to go on every day; even these must be extremely bloody, though nothing but the sites and numbers are reported. I inscribe the place names on the familiar map unrolled in my dim memory and wonder whether those are accidental skirmishes or the outcome of careful planning. Is it an isolated incident or a sign of something?

We sit in the shade of geraniums, crack eggs, spread rose jam on bread, and eat slowly. I read the newspaper, sometimes check my finger, and then move it again. I can sometimes see the face of the macabre, or sometimes just its profile, but its eyes, its wounds are never visible. It cannot even climb over a piece of bread to reach me. Concepts occur to me, one after another, but while I fumble with them, their flesh crumbles, their vital fluid spills, and they become mere empty shells. I don't even have to reach out my fingers; they turn hollow right before my eyes.

She reads the international wire services from one end to the other, then slowly breaks off a piece of bread, spreads butter and jam on it, and carries it to her mouth. Her cheeks

(180

move and I can just hear the muffled sound of her teeth masticating the crust.

She casts a sharp, challenging look at me.

"There's no mention of a third offensive anywhere. It wasn't talked about yesterday or today, either. According to your story, it should come on some kind of a holiday or around a holiday, on a Saturday night and especially a moonless Saturday night. But there seem to be nothing but reports of small skirmishes. I wonder if it isn't all your imagination, little turd?"

"It may be, but lying low and being dormant are two very different things. The movement is *there*, whether you can see it or not; they are always moving over there. Certain groups especially. They are not idle and they don't permit others to be either. Whenever they receive a stimulus, they can reach out in any direction in response. If there is no stimulus, they will create one and continue to move and to grow. Besides, speaking of skirmishes, the tactical move I described was also a skirmish. Even in the local paper, the battle I told you about was a matter of several lines at most. It wasn't even worth a filler item for foreign correspondents. But when one phase of the battle was over, we counted heads and found out that two hundred men had been reduced to seventeen. I was one of them, one seventeenth."

She falls silent and looks away; stabbing the belly of the round bread with a knife and turning it around, she splits it into two and paints it with jam. I wipe off my glasses with my shirt sleeve and continue to read the newspaper.

While I read, I have the feeling that I am doing something constructive, but as soon as I finish, the feeling disappears, and the realization comes over me that the vacation is over. I have not been approached by anyone, I have never committed myself to anyone, and I have no contract with any news service. This may be a habit left over from the time when I was playing at being a special overseas correspondent. Somehow I seem to have created a distant but permanent stage set. It fades immediately, but it never completely disappears and is always drifting just behind my ear or somewhere in that vicinity. I finish eating and put down the paper, then I feel empty, and go out with her for a walk. The city, dominated by glass, steel, and concrete, soars and gleams in the light of summer, which has passed its prime and begun to fade. Along the sidewalk, perfume bottles sparkle in the red, gold, and black of the glass boxes, and multitudes of tourists go past us in buses, on their way to see the wall. They cross over to the other side and look at the roads and buildings through the window without getting out of the bus and return to this side. In the aquarium, a monster catfish, almost three yards long, glares, his small eyes covered with opaque white film, and breathes heavily. Under a sturdy chestnut tree in the zoo, a band is playing "When the Saints Go Marching In" with gaudy sweetness and an old woman is selling oats for pigeon feed. As I spill some of the oats at my feet while I sit drinking a beer, a large flock of pigeons overwhelms me like an avalanche. One of them waddles toward the oats, and at every step sooty sparrows swiftly cut ahead of him and snatch the feed.

"What happens when the third offensive comes?"

"They will probably be fighting in the cities."

"What will really happen?"

"Big skirmishes, probably."

"Are you going to the front again?"

"I don't know. I'll decide that at the time, once I'm over there. I'm not going to plan anything beforehand. I may go, or I may stay in my room, trembling."

"You are not safe in the room either, are you?"

"I suppose not. There's no inside or outside over there. Judging by Tet and May, a tremendous number of houses were destroyed. They invaded from the suburbs, and the outskirts and slums became the battlefields. Both sides used heavy equipment, and helicopters showered rockets from the sky. Many people died, probably while hiding under their houses. There's no difference between 'in' or 'out.' Everything is total war. Over there, they call it 'dying violently in bed.' I heard it many times. Those people have clever expressions."

"You sound as though you've already decided to go."

I spill some more oats on the table, push them to the edge, and drop some water on them. Pigeons and sparrows flutter down in an uproar, hopping and jostling one another on the table. The sparrows fly busily onto my hand, pierce my skin with their claws, and thrust out their heads. Pigeons waddle clumsily between the glasses filled with beer. They have corpulent, heavy bodies and do not have the delicate resilience of sparrows. Even if I die, the pigeons will be here just the same, every day . . . This thought suddenly flashed through my mind and disappeared, overshadowing a considerable area of my consciousness. I waited for the ground to cave in; but I only heard a distant rumble in my ear, in the hazy but dazzling sun.

Gazing at the pigeons, she suddenly cried: "Let's go pike fishing!"

She went on quietly in a soft voice: "There are any number of planes, every day. We can go back to the hotel now and tell them by phone that we're checking out and pack, then we can leave in thirty minutes. Take off. We have a map, plenty of information, and a lake system. That area is full of pastures and lakes and I have been there once already. There's nowhere I haven't been in this country. So, let's go, please.

Forget about a war in another country. No one really takes it as seriously as they say they do. If they did, they wouldn't be able to sleep. The reason that everyone talks about it so loudly is because it's far away and involves other people. Everyone wants to talk about other people's political problems; the farther the country, the more simply and heroically they can talk. When it comes to their own country, they are frightened to talk about the tiniest tremor and they begin to stutter right away. It's true. In other words, they can suffer without dirtying their hands, which is an attraction. They can speak eloquently without being held responsible and they won't be killed by either side. It's very appealing. And if you go over there, taking your life in your own hands, and find out the truth, both the left and the right will read into your account only what they choose to find there and they'll use it for propaganda and turn it to their own advantage. The rest won't matter at all. If they used it at all, it would at least be something; but by now, everyone thinks the topic is *passé* and no one wants to read about it. Everyone talks about it because the United States is still in it, but if they pull out, no one will give a damn. There are all sorts of bloody battles all over the world and they are just as atrocious and just as treacherous, but no one says anything about them; in other words, it's pure theater. They only come in flocks to see the great actors on stage, and they can't be bothered the rest of the time. So, little turd, give it up this time. Worrying and fussing about it all by yourself won't save anything. It's nothing but an expendable item in history. You know this very well, but you are too stupid to save yourself. Let's go to the lake and fish for pike, and you can teach me how to cast, too."

She glanced up at me as she talked and then averted her eyes. For some time she looked at the pigeons in silence, and then she began to speak again, casting a glance at me from time to time. There was an air of knowingness about her that was the result of repeated efforts at self-control, deliberation, and observation, and her wisdom held a hint of resignation, and I detected an aimless passion as well. And, somehow, when she lowered her head, her hair and her neck exuded unhappiness, as if acid had been spilled from a bottle.

At night, we turned the dark corner by the pipe shop onto the boulevard. There was a Chinese restaurant with a sign-board reading "South China." Suddenly the darkness changed to red, gold, and black. The sharp, urgent, high voice of a girl singing echoed constantly from the walls of this small eating place. Everywhere, on the wall and on the pillars, there were "Great Happiness" hangings, and thick, golden calligraphy written on red Chinese paper was used for the wall decoration. She was cheered by a dry martini and was happy to read the writing aloud.

"South of the pavilion
    Where the wine tastes sweet and green plums are ripe,
It's Chinese summer
    When food is delicious and pearly grains are fragrant.

"You can't beat the Chinese poets," she said. "They always cheer me up, and yet they are so dignified. Professor Chao has a hanging written by his wife. It goes:

Live long like the eternal green pines of the southern
    mountain,
Be happy as the long current of the Northern Sea.

The verses are banal but her calligraphy is magnificent. Still, I like this better; it gives me an appetite. Of course, you would like to change the phrase 'pearly grains are fragrant' into 'my "pearly gate" is fragrant.' "

She sipped her martini and laughed aloud, mischievously stuck out the tip of her tongue, and shrugged her shoulders. Her high cheek bones were tinged with pink and she gazed at me with her usual look, having its hint of a wry smile. She lowered the glass and put her smiling face close to mine, looking into my eyes.

"Is my pearly gate fragrant?"

She asked with an air of concern; as soon as the words dropped from her mouth, she pulled back, and stared, looking arrogant and aloof, at a black lacquer screen encrusted with delicately gleaming mother-of-pearl.

After the meal, I was feeling replete, drinking jasmine tea and rinsing the oil from my lips and tongue, when she stealthily put out her hand and took away my Zippo lighter. It was covered with scratches, grimy with oil and soot, and the silver plating had peeled off here and there, showing the yellow metal underneath. The lighter fluid leaked a little and stained my pocket, but it still worked well and it had become an extension of my hand; I have carried it with me for years. There are some words, scratched on each side. She squinted at it and scrutinized the writing.

"What does this mean? It says, or rather it seems to read 'Troi dat oil.' What language is it?"

"It's their language over there. It's pronounced '*Choi dot'oi*' and it sounds like the Japanese '*Cho dokkoi*'—Hold on! In Vietnamese, literally translated, it means something like 'Ah, God in Heaven and God on Earth.' There is also 'Troi oi.' I think that means one of the gods, either of Heaven or Earth, I've forgotten which."

"This side is in English. It's long. 'Yea though I walk through the valley of the shadow of death I will fear no evil for I am the evilest son of a bitch in the valley.' What does it mean? I don't understand at all."

"It's a charm for evading bullets. They believe that if you carve these words on your lighter you won't get hit. It's an American soldiers' charm. Soldiers are the same the world over, they all are superstitious about talismans, because they have nothing else to depend on. So, I asked them to carve it for me, too."

"Did you take it to the jungle?"

"Yes."

"You've been carrying it around ever since?"

"That's right."

"Next to your skin?"

"Yes."

She handed back the lighter in silence. Her expression, which had been open a moment ago, suddenly closed up completely and her wry smile vanished. Her eyes grew hollow, and she drew in her cheeks sharply. Surely she had seen the lighter before this at the lake, in the room, by my pillow morning and night, everywhere. This object, to which she had never paid any attention, suddenly took on enormous significance for her. Astonished, she looked into her teacup and found that she was gazing at her rejected self. As always, the final truth of an experience casts a warning shadow before it in minute detail; but we forget. We are infatuated by the whole truth, only to be put off eventually by details; or we become too attached to the details and are destroyed by truth itself.

Returning to the room, I open the window, sit down, and take out a half-crushed paper carton from my knapsack. I arrange fur, thread, nail clippers, and a small bottle of adhesive on the table and begin to wind the artificial flies. She changes into a negligée, lies down in bed, and reads the newspaper or a weekly magazine, but she soon throws it away and begins to talk. She gets out of bed, folds her arms under her voluptuous breasts, and leaning against the bleak, dark wall, opens her mouth. She begins to murmur in a low voice, without hatred, without abuse, but insistently. I could smell it from the beginning, she says. You are a stupid man; stupid and clumsy, but I didn't realize that. You can't escape yourself. All this time we have been together, just the two of us, and you didn't see anyone, didn't go out, didn't even leave the apartment for a walk. I often suggested having a pizza party for Professor Steinkopf but you resented it. Once or twice you came along to the seminar room at the University, but very reluctantly, only from a sense of duty. The rest of the time you locked yourself up in the apartment and slept all day. Sleep and eat, eat and sleep; that was all. If anyone appeared, you were so frightened—you once hid in the kitchen, didn't you? You felt threatened by my hysteria and went to the lake to catch pike, but you were still avoiding the necessity of meeting and talking to people. But when we got here, and you heard about the third offensive, what did you do? You dashed out all by yourself and went to wire service people you didn't know from Adam and coolly flashed your obsolete army identification and looked through the telex files, didn't you? Without any rest for hours on end, what's more. I'm simply flabbergasted. When I say I smell it, I'm referring to your attitude. You were totally fulfilled and alive. You were excited and as full of energy as a child—that is what I meant. Didn't you leave Tokyo to get hold of this news somewhere, rather than see me? While you were sleeping with me, weren't you staring over my ass, waiting for something to happen? I was just a restaurant at a railroad junction and you were killing time until the next train; isn't that it? I wouldn't put anything past you, you probably read about the first and second offensives in Tokyo; you suspected the third, and I bet you signed an exclusive contract with some newspaper and came rushing out of

Japan. You stink; I can smell you from miles away. Admit it; get it out of your system!

That's not true, I protest. There's a misunderstanding. It was pure coincidence. If you hadn't read the newspaper that morning, nothing would have happened. I would be fishing for pike by now. It's true. I knew about the first and the second offensives, but I hadn't expected the third one. Even now, I'm only half convinced. Don't you understand? If that were my intention, I wouldn't be here, would I? I would've gone over there long ago to wait. I would be sleeping, reading, and drinking in an apartment room with sandbags piled up in it like an air raid shelter, and we would be telling each other dirty jokes from morning to night. *Chi chi cognac* and *bok bok soda*. What on earth is that? It's cognac and soda, I answer. A little cognac and a lot of soda. We drink it and chatter like baboons behind the sandbags. Foreign languages when spoken by the Japanese sound terrible, but theirs is peculiar too. "No can do," they say; it means there's nothing one can do, or that's the end of a chapter, and it's used when you don't know what to do. They use *fini*, too. Also *troi oi*. I explained to you about *Troi dat oi*. The situation is *no can do, fini,* and *troi oi* and ends up as *Dinky dau*. This means crazy.

Don't be funny, she says. You can't pull the wool over my eyes; I don't know whether it's *chichi* or *bokbok,* and let's forget about the special contract with the newspapers and say you got interested because I happened to read the newspaper. That might have been a coincidence, I admit. But the point is that you jumped at it. You immediately changed a coincidence into an inevitability; that is what I am talking about. Your sense of inevitability was frustrated, it kept complaining that one card was short, that something somewhere was missing. So you tried sleeping with me, catching pike, and doing all sorts of things, but nothing filled the vacuum. Then suddenly

(189

you drew an ace. You snatched it without even examining your hand. And now, you can never, never part with it. I am a station restaurant, a pizza snack. You never loved me from the beginning. I told you this once. You are incapable of loving—not just a woman; you can't even love yourself. So you go looking for danger. You are a hollow explorer. You will do anything or go anywhere to fill the vacuum. You can't be satisfied with an abstract idea. You don't like to "creep into bed and choke on your own wind," as the philosopher said. But you don't know what to do, so you try to rent other people's passion. I've heard that tapirs eat bad dreams, but you set out to eat other people's passion, and you'd do anything for it. You charge blindly in one mad rush. You are like a flame of ice, and I must admit that I admire you for it. But no matter how many times you slept with me, you were only sleeping with an object. You tried to pretend, but you cooled off right away. What do you really want to do over there? Smoke opium?

I wouldn't mind trying opium once more, I say. "Over there" is a distant country you don't know, so I will use this place as an example, since you know it better than I do. This place is divided by a wall into East and West and on either side they call the opposite side "over there." To the east, the wall is a bulwark against fascism; to the west, it's the wall of a prison. The children in the East bring bouquets of appreciation to the sentries, while in the West they take wreaths for the dead who were shot trying to climb over. I am not involved on either side. Neither here nor over there. I can't pretend to be involved when I am not. People who want to can pretend that they are, but I can't do that. I've been forced to realize the appalling gulf between those who are in it and those who are outside. So, whether it's here or over there, my position is neither east nor west of the wall. If I can see east,

I see the East, if I can look west, I look at the West. I watch the wall and the sky too. There must be facts that only the people in the East can grasp, and other facts that only the Westerners can discover. Both sides claim to know the whole truth. But there must be other facts that only the men on the wall itself can understand. That is also an entity. I don't know of any "unique" reality. All I can see are facts. If I can survive and write something, both sides will take from it whatever is convenient for them and use it to justify their own position. You are right in saying that if they find out that they can't use it, they will sneer at it, slander it, or ignore it. While they can use it, either or both sides will welcome it, but after that, it will be thrown out. They claim that there is only one truth, but when they are in a predicament, they use an unbiased third party as their witness. They are all expedience. You said that the attraction of distant countries' political problems is being able to suffer without getting dirty yourself, which is very true. If you are not in the situation of killing or being killed, you can talk or argue about anything.

It doesn't matter, she says. If you can't love me, that's all right too. Only stay for another month as we are now. I just need time. Please. After that, you can go whenever you want; I need time to prepare myself. This is too cruel, a station restaurant, a snack. Please put up with me just a little longer and stay with me. I've really dropped pretty low saying such things, and I know very well you will think I'm disgusting. You don't have to tell me, I know. If you want to run away, say it right out. Say "I've had enough of you, goodbye." I'm accustomed to being jilted. I've done some jilting, too. It only means the turn of the tide. Only it came too suddenly. That's all.

Her cheeks were sunken, her face pale, and her eyes were like fish eyes, shiny and yet hollow, both brilliant and shocked at the same time. The bloom on her flesh was gone. The young girl who clapped her hands and danced in the meadow in the evening twilight had disappeared. So had the superb housewife. Suddenly she had aged ten years and was wallowing in a bleak, cynical desolation. She seemed unaware of the fact that it was her incomparable aim that had brought the catastrophe on herself. She was totally clear-headed and yet extremely hazy. Suddenly she seemed to expand. She grew larger and larger until she overflowed her own frame and filled the room, blocking every nook and cranny. She got off the bed and moved lifelessly across the room; after washing her face and fumbling with her hair, she returned to bed. She crossed her legs, gazed at the corns on the sole of her foot, idly picked up the newspaper, fell on her back, and began to read the fashion page.

I didn't dare raise my eyes, so I concentrated on the artificial flies, trimming off excess fur or tying the thread firmly. I was uncomfortable to the point of suffocation, and I felt my disgust spread over everything. She had been completely right in her accusation and her attack was merciless. It was like being exposed under the lights of an operating theater. I could not blink my eyes, I could not shield them; I just froze in bewilderment. When she read the news to me, didn't I feel that I had found my hidden clue? Didn't I sense something long awaited suddenly taking shape? Didn't I feel exhilarated because I knew instantly that I could leave, that I could escape?

She put down the newspaper and rose from the bed.

"Is it opium, or a woman?" she asked, glancing at me sharply. "Don't hide it, tell me the truth."

After dawdling a little, she looked at her corns again and sighed audibly, then fell into bed once more. Showing her round back to me and keeping her face turned away, she said in a voice that was too high to be talking to herself:

"It was going so well at the lake, or rather I thought it was going well. It's absurd that I should be tricked into getting so deeply involved! I believed you. It's a big joke; it's like a popular song. I didn't realize that I was in the category of station restaurant. I've really grown dull. I wasted one whole summer. If I had known it was going to be like this, I would have gone with Professor Steinkopf." She clacked her tongue angrily.

It may be that I don't even love myself. It is just as she says. I can't even love a woman out of conceit. I am frightened of myself, wretched; rather than build something constructive, I am bent on throwing it away. I seem to remember having said to her that as long as I could not forget myself, I could not possibly escape myself either. In this day and age, when there is no such thing as a journey, merely transition, departure must be an obsolete concept. Must I live with her for another month, threatened all the time by moments of collapse and total alienation, embracing my lethargic inner turmoil? Am I to be swallowed up by the bed, getting steadily fatter, covered by monstrous leaves, growing vines, and extending the roots of my sickness, dusted by the dry powder of what was my vital fluid? She was a veteran hunter who could memorize the total topography with one glance at those areas in herself that overlapped with me. Without having to lift a finger, she smelled me out by a stirring of the breeze, drove me out of the bush, and cornered me in front of the cliff. But she doesn't seem to feel or understand anything in those areas where she had no previous experience. Her power to absorb me springs from the past we share, but when I told her of my own past experiences, it did not seem to have enough impact to disturb even a leaf. Although my memories had been edited and revised so much over the years that they obviously retained none of their original form, I did make an effort to transform what seeped to the surface of my skin into words, as faithfully as I could. But after listening to me, she said nothing. Nothing came to life in her cheeks or in her eyes. She stretched out her heavy bare arms in the light of the little reading lamp, and looked at them silently from various angles. I felt as though I had breathed words into an empty bottle and thrown it in the ocean without even corking it. If one only talks about what is fact, it is mere chatter. Chatter is chatter. The more I talked about it all, the more the facts receded and became ambiguous. All my words were worm-riddled. A solitude smeared by fingerprints seemed to shroud my torso. Disgust welled up in me as I talked. I was irritated and more than once had an impulse just to stop saying anything. What bothered me more than anything else was the fact that the memories had turned into something that could be articulated not just tens, but hundreds, of times, something that I could describe to someone else. I could enjoy a drink while I talked about it. An experience is an independent entity, but its shell only crumbles into finer and finer dust the more one fingers it. I felt as though I was circling around and around an island that did not appear on any map, was trapped in the tidal whirlpool, unable to come one inch closer to the shore, although I could see every detail of the forests on the slopes, the rivers, and the shoreline.

In order to witness the possible Saturday night attack, I would have to catch a flight heading south on Thursday or Friday, but I could reserve a seat at any time by picking up the phone. I decided to believe this was possible and dawdled, reading the newspaper and drinking beer. I spent the latter half of the week in my chair, getting fat. August had come to an end. A new week had begun, but it was dull and mediocre; there was nothing to distinguish it from any other week. The sun fades more and more, and when I walk through the forest on the outskirts of the city, I can see the desolate wraith of autumn rise from the grasses, shadows, and tree trunks and secretly wander ahead of me. I wait for her while she amuses herself picking toadstools, and the chill of the air bites into my forehead and hands. She comes anywhere with me if I invite her, but she is pale, her flesh has shrunk, and she has become taciturn. All the cheerful sharp wit and sensitivity, all those things in which she indulged herself all summer have vanished. The shape of her actions and words has become vague, almost invisible, sluggish and lethargic. After having a meal at the South China, we return to the room. When I watch her turn on the light, open the windows, or walk slowly across the room, I sometimes feel like calling out to her. But we have both closed up physically, and we retreat within ourselves, stealing a glance at each other. At times I wonder whether we are avoiding or stalking each other. I devote myself to making artificial flies, but I am afraid of running out of material, and take each one apart with a razor blade after so carefully completing it. I start all over again from scratch. Sitting by the window, I repeat the motions of finishing it and taking it apart, assembling and disassembling it. She has expanded all over the room and fills the air to the point of suffocation, but there is something about her like a cargo newly arrived at the warehouse. She seems to be isolated from the wall, from the bed, and sometimes even from her negligée. Her shoes, toothbrush, suitcases, are all independent of her. When she touches them languorously, they flock around her; but when her hands let them go, the bond is undone and they become mere individual pieces.

She gets up aimlessly and talks to me in a faint, gloomy

voice, dangling her legs from the bed, hunching her shoulders, and jutting out her chin like a convalescent.

"What are all your friends doing?" she asks.

"I seldom ever see them these days."

"They are all settled as family men, living bored but solid lives. No one is looking around hungrily like you. You seem to be scornful of them, but this is no small achievement. It's like growing a shell around a pearl."

"Not at all! I don't despise them! That's another misunderstanding. The only thing is that I couldn't stand it. If I settle down I feel as though I am going to rot from my head on down. All I can do every morning is to work out how to dodge the day. I am weak; I am fragile."

"What childish things are you babbling about at your age? If that's an excuse, it's a pretty shabby one. You really have demeaned yourself. You took a vacation but you are being henpecked by a woman, and just because you don't know how to say goodbye, you are wasting each day. It serves you right. I won't let you say goodbye. Stay tied down here for a long time!"

"Well . . . the ones who stayed at university are assistant professors by now, and those who succeeded to their fathers'. businesses are presidents. At the news service, they are desk head or deputy department chief. They have all grown fat or bald, and their faces are so completely changed that I can't tell them apart. If they get together, they talk about sickness or golf. Diabetes and blood pressure are popular topics. If you start to talk about illness, they come alive. Another subject to talk about is During the War, when they were children and ate horse fodder like pressed beans and weeds—that's another good conversational gambit. You can talk about it for hours on end. If they are forbidden to talk about sickness and pressed beans, it's as good as tying their hands behind their backs and throwing them into a river. Pressed beans are a particularly good subject. You can really be carried away by it. Our generation's fetish is the bean cake; it's the holy Mecca, nothing else will do."

"So, just because you're afraid you'll rot, you continually spin like a top. You think that as long as you keep spinning you'll stay upright, but that if you stop you'll fall over. Nobody has asked you, but you want to go over there and die like a dog behind a garbage dump and I suppose that's your dream come true. Congratulations! It serves you right."

Groping in her hair with the tips of her pale fingers, she turned her face to me. Her hair covered her face completely and through it her eyes glared brilliantly; she had chewed her lips, leaving visible marks of her contempt. She looked like an angry snake rearing its head. Would she scream or attack me? I put down the artificial flies and stared at her. She was pushed to the limit of her endurance and beyond. Yet, for some unknown reason, she retreated. Her eyes covered with hair, she rolled back into bed like a parcel.

I too am alienated. I take up the artificial fly and begin to wind it, but I can't lose myself in the fur or the hook. I can't braid them; I can't tie them, nor can I stabilize them. I can't complete the fly, but I can't undo it either. The flies open and fall like butterflies or flowers under my eyes, but I cannot muster the necessary concentration. In the cold breeze of the late summer night, within these walls that turn incessantly from red to blue, in time with the Coca-Cola signs, I don't know how to prepare for death behind the garbage dump. I cannot leave here with this ambiguity. I sit back and get fat, warm and plumped with Schnapps, and my brains rot away. I am swallowed up by the bed, glued to the wrinkles in the sheets, and cannot even embrace her. I become a delicate, puffed-up caterpillar that exerts itself only to pick up a book or a newspaper or a fork. Here, people were shot to death trying to climb over the wall from east to west, trying to dig a tunnel under the wall, or jumping from the windows of a building by the wall. They were shot trying to swim across the canal, and trying to run to the old tram car going to the west. But there is no wire mesh over the restaurant windows to guard against hand grenades. There are no machine guns at the hotel entrances, no sandbag barricades around the beds. They don't cook wild rats in a washbasin for food. Middle-school teachers are not shot through the head from behind during their lunch hour by female noodle vendors, and they don't sleep with their shoes on in canvas cots, waiting for the trench mortars that may shower shells over their heads at any moment. I don't know what sources of determination I have available. Over there, I could gather it from anything, just like a bee; but now, my belly has gone soft. It has grown tender from eating rich food, from sex, and useless soul-searching. My body sags under the mere weight of my internal monologues, and it is beyond the capacity of my feet to carry it. Fragments of words and phrases from countless books I had once pored over and devoured like a bookworm hover constantly in my head; they jab me ferociously in certain spots, or gnaw into my bones. Pairs of antonyms bite into me simultaneously with perfectly balanced force and depth; they either begin to make me feel driven or else soporific. A silly story. Even at this point, I am bound by other people's words. It's just as she says, I am drowning in a blanket pulled up to my chin, choking on my own wind.

Sometimes, fear looms up, raising its broad, cold, wet back, and then as I watch, petrified, it gradually sinks back again. Inevitably, I try to remember deathbeds, the bags of flesh that were almost totally destroyed but still alive, or the flesh that had solidified into a mere thing, the things I witnessed on the levees, in hospital morgues, bombed-out bars, and jungles; but they are all hazy and useless. If I put them into words, they may momentarily come alive and frighten her, but I know only too well that words are nothing but hollow shells. Behind her rigid back, I will be collapsed and limp. If I saw here and now what I have seen over there, I would probably lose my voice. Corpses are always awkward, intensely vivid, vulgar, shabby. No matter how often I see them, I shall never be able to overcome my fear. When the strange feelings begin to encroach, I stiffen and fall silent, or try to relieve the stiffness and smile, or suddenly burst out laughing to relieve the others present who are in the same condition I'm in. I may talk about the surroundings of the object I fear with hushed awe, or discuss it instead of uttering the usual amenities, or worry over how to talk about it. Thus I try to break down the object of my fear with countless small, clumsy attempts at actions and words. But living things are constantly moving. The flow of living matter destroys and encroaches and fears, too, flow like living matter. Talk is syphilis; self-knowledge is syphilis. To me, peace is syphilis. These are intangible and unavoidable things that secretly and tenaciously try to rot me away and force me down into my chair. Fat mounds up thickly on my withered, softened belly, forming a bulge and spilling over. I touch it, and look at the woman's body sprawling on the bed, and wind my artificial flies.

To go to the toilet, I must get off the bed, slip shoes onto my feet, open the door, and walk out into the long, dark corridor. The corridor is as old-fashioned as the room and has a high ceiling; the darkness begins at chest height, and I cannot see the ceiling if I look up. The toilet bowl and the bathtub are both large and sturdy, broad, thick, and covered with scars.

She takes a bath, returns to the room and talks to the

mirror in a somewhat softened voice: "I just realized; having had experiences like that, you must feel most things are absurd and you probably can't take anything seriously. That was probably why you did nothing but sleep all the time. And I began to think that I was foolish to be irritated by it. I suddenly realized. The hot water didn't run properly and I couldn't get warm."

She spoke with tenderness, and sounded cheerful, coquettish, and apologetic, but when I looked at her profile as she slid into the bed, her cheeks were etched into hollows and she was biting her lips. Shadows that I had never seen before had appeared under her eyes. She patted her pillow a little to puff it up, fell silent again, and sank into the sheets.

I tried to remember the large cavity in which I could see lungs moving at every slow breath, the green combat uniform that soaked up blood like spreading black ink, and those dark eyes that gazed into my hands lighting a cigarette. The wounded watched me without agonizing or crying, as if basking in the sun. These memories flash and disappear. By the incessant handling we call reminiscence, they are so damaged that they are unable to climb over the artificial flies to come to me; their eyes and mouths are lost in a blur. And even when they are recalled and come quite close to me, they are separated from me by fog, and just stand still, quite lost. If I try to use concentration to call them to my side, the contrary happens and they become hazy, ephemeral, and finally invisible. Not wanting to be hindered by a breeze or a wall, I try to commune with the night, to borrow its power and arm myself with a hard carapace, but the more I try, the more I go as limp as the flesh of a clam pried from its shell. I did not want to be distracted by the breeze, by the flashing walls, by the mushrooms in the woods, or by her soft, deliberately audible sighs. But my fears disappeared, leaving mere effigies if I pursued them directly. Nevertheless, the moment I dropped my guard, they returned and attacked me ruthlessly. I would be in the midst of urinating into the bowl with its network of large yellow cracks, or of walking slowly down the dark corridor, close to the wall. They crushed me instantly at a blow and I had a flashing glimpse of something that froze my heart. I fled into the darkness.

The fear assaults me late at night, too. The tide seems to be rising again. They seem to be waiting, stalking me. When I am in bed, somewhere, suddenly, an enormous earthquake occurs. An intense shock runs through me. My body almost jumps off the mattress. An avalanche storms past me. I see it gouge the surface of the earth, tearing up trees, stones, and soft soil with its scythe, and then disappear. Recollections, self-examinations, the scalding guilt that follows an act of soul-searching, and the imagination, premonition, and idle thoughts that shimmer beyond them—everything is swept soundlessly away. My hands and feet are paralyzed and I cannot move. Cold perspiration sometimes oozes from me. The bed, the wall, and the city fade away, and a vast darkness rises from my feet, expanding into infinity. Rigid with fear, I gaze into the desolation and the stillness. I was often attacked by this feeling in my student days, and since then a total disintegration has occurred with every bout. I tried to explain it by thinking that an overwhelming fear generated an excessive sense of vitality that left my body behind, causing a vacuum and alienation. But actually I was emphasizing the ideas of "excess" and "life force" rather than explaining the phenomenon itself. And this argument was a determined self-deception stirred by my desire not to recognize my incapacity; so, for a time, I prided myself on this explanation, relying on it completely, but when I realized that no amount of resistance would save me from defeat, the entire phenomenon gradually disappeared. Now, when I need to muster up my determination, I concentrate on recollection of devastation and atrocity; this may have triggered everything again. After a deep trauma, reminiscence feels like a temporary illusion. It comes at any time. The lake fades away and the *Abendrot* dissipates. The sparkling fish vanish, and the hayloft disappears. The glass walls melt away and the leather couch evaporates. Solitude spreads everywhere, and is diffused throughout my body. My bones and entrails dissolve and I cannot even feel the skin. I also used to experience solitude in the echoes of sleep and the effect of opium, but then there was a pure, pellucid, reassuring vacuum in it. In contrast, this vacuum contains only a freezing expanse of nothingness and I tremble like an orphan.

One evening she went out to buy cigarettes, and when she returned to the room she diffidently put the package on the table. "Just now, when I was walking along out there," she murmured, "I heard glass shatter in my head."

She glanced at me with bewildered eyes and quietly began to change her clothes. After taking off her slacks, she seemed to run out of energy and slipped into bed as she was.

After a while, with her face averted, she said: "Hold me. Come here and hold me." She begged me. The thin, faint voice held a strange note. I hurried into bed and embraced her gently from behind. She clasped my hand, or rather, merely brushed it. Her touch was a little clammy and cold, and she had no strength anywhere in her fingers. It seemed as if she might collapse at any moment. Her face was buried in the pillow, and she was trembling all over. She quieted down after a while, but she was like a sodden straw in water; then resilience began to flow back into various parts of her body and she started to quiver.

A muffled voice spoke into the pillow: "I don't want to become like my mother."

Again, she murmured vaguely: "I don't want to become like Mother."

Her voice had no force. She seemed to have spent all her capacity for calling up passion, and exhausted her suffering. A weakness had surfaced that I had never seen or imagined in her. Rather than holding onto these words in case she lost herself completely, she seemed to be already floating in some strange, foreign realm. Fear shot through me. My hands, feet, and chest suddenly went cold. My hand almost slipped off her shoulder.

"What is it? What about your mother?"

I held her and turned her around. She looked up obediently, her head flopping on the pillow. I looked into her face and saw devastation in it. There was no explosive regret like the other days' to be seen. She was merely pale, her lips a little parted, and deep lines were etched into an expression of rare peace. I had never asked her questions or pried deeper into her stories unless she told me of her own accord. I wondered if her mother had been a foreigner. I wondered if the scent of misfortune that shrouded her originated from this. I wondered whether she had been supporting her mother during some period of her girlhood when she was a *ku ai tzu*. I had wondered what would have been inevitable in her life in order for her to achieve this. Was my wild guess right? And if so, was this the reason that she was able to hate Japan so passionately?

Suddenly, she came back to me. Her face was no longer a wilderness. Her eyes came into focus and glistened serenely; looking at me, she gave a wry smile.

"Did I say something?"

"No. You didn't say anything."

"Really?"

"You just didn't feel well."

"After I bought the cigarettes, I was walking down the street, and suddenly I heard glass crashing in my head. So I hurried back, but I felt terribly dizzy and I lost consciousness. For some reason, I feel exhausted, so I'm going to sleep for a bit."

Moving wearily, she slowly changed into a negligée and mouthed a silent goodnight; no sooner had she muttered that she had a mild headache than she began to breathe softly in her sleep.

After about an hour, she woke up and said that she wanted something delicious to eat, that she wanted to go to the South China and eat a good chop suey. A bright light was shining in the pipe shop on the corner, and I caught a glimpse through the window of the cork wall covered from floor to ceiling with innumerable pipes, all shining like brown gems. The South China, all in red, gold, and black, was full of customers with sparkling, damp, light-blue eyes, perspiring bald heads, and shiny, rosy cheeks. There was only one empty table behind the screen encrusted with mother of pearl, so we sat there facing each other. We ordered two super-dry martinis and from the paltry menu (which was out of keeping with the arrogantly polite face of the waiter), we ordered jellyfish and pig's stomach for hors d'oeuvres, shark's fin and egg white soup, and chop suey and fried shrimp balls for the main course. Chop suey is a symphony of food scraps and the word can be written using various Chinese characters. At this restaurant, it was called *pa-po-tsai*, or eight treasured vegetables. I tore a page from my notebook and wrote *Chuan-chia-fu*, or "the happiness of the entire family," and gave it to the waiter, but he seemed unable to read the Chinese characters, although he was unmistakably Chinese. He took the piece of paper to the kitchen and disappeared, and soon, with a melting smile, brought out rice mixed and fried in sesame oil with all the kitchen leftovers. If it had only been called a Chinese dish because of the smell of sesame oil instead of butter, I would have had to acknowledge the point; but it was more like horse fodder than human food. She narrowed her eyes and ate copiously, exclaiming that it was delicious. I ate about half, without comment. The restaurant had Chinese workers, but evidently no cook.

South of the pavilion
    Where the wine tastes sweet and green plums are ripe,
It's Chinese summer
    When food is delicious and pearly grains are fragrant.

"Even I can cook something like this," I said. "It's a fried hodgepodge of all the leftover vegetables, goulash à la student. If they can make money out of this, anything goes. If you served this sort of thing in Hong Kong, coolies would beat the hell out of you. The coolies at the Hong Kong harbors are eating sumptuous leftovers. Try sipping a porridge of innards behind a garbage dump. It's an oasis of peace in the midst of chaos. I wonder where the Chinese here come from."

"I know, I know, I understand. Please don't speak so loudly. I'm quite satisfied with it. Even this is a great treat for me. I said all sorts of unpleasant things to you, but you have treated me royally. I want to apologize."

Her voice suddenly tapered off, and I hastily prepared myself for tears. She had been like that all day, since the incident. As I stared through the mixture of faintly salty olive and bitter, chilled gin, blood began to color in her high cheeks, but her shoulders and neck had lost their usual alert, insolent set. The girl standing in the boat who slapped her arms, the woman who slowly paraded in front of the mirror draping a sealskin coat over her nude body, both disappeared. The cold alcohol and the hot food lit snow lanterns in her cheeks. Visible only from the waist up across the white table-cloth, she rested her arms on the cloth and lowered her eyes; she looked solemn, but nothing like she had the night before. The turbulent stream with its slowly moving eddies, the shallows sparkling in the sun, the unexpectedly dark, rich pool, and the clear waterfall that threw up sluggishly trembling yellow foam—all the things that she represented disappeared and her eyes, shoulders, and arms took on the light of the winter sun. Everything was pale, withered, limp, and cold. She was like a deer shot in the pelvis; whose legs had collapsed and yet who was innocently looking up, unaware of what had happened to her.

She did not raise her eyes, but stared down as if she were examining the back of her head from the inside rather than the rim of the plate. She murmured:

"When I was a child, I once read a fisherman's song in an illustrated book, Scottish or Indonesian, it doesn't matter. It goes like this:

> For men must work
> And women must weep.

In the end it all comes back to this. The more things change, the more they stay the same. I now understand what that saying is all about. I suddenly realized at the tobacco shop. And I felt faint. I don't know whether you are going over there intending to work, but in the end you will have to. You are inured to cruelty but you are so inexperienced in kindness. I won't pursue you any more, you are free to go wherever you want."

She murmured these words with a certain evident detachment that was neither resigned nor supercilious. She sipped the two or three drops that remained at the bottom of the martini glass and made a faint but noticeable grimace. She spoke gently but my trauma had already begun. Suddenly I felt that I was being forced to stand on the very edge of a diving board above a pool, while something stared at me from behind. Now that I was free of her, and had obtained what I wanted, I should have been exhilarated; yet there was nothing but alienation. She was silhouetted against the red darkness of a foreign land and I did not know when she would vanish into it; perhaps as much as half of her body had already been claimed, but she gazed into the ashtray with clear dark eyes. She was not being swallowed up by that strange land. Wasn't I sheltering under her broad wings, leaving only my face exposed, at the same time that I was struggling to escape from her? When I thought about it, I almost collapsed. I was confusion itself, and yet bent on imitating sanity, while she was half insane, and yet remained magnanimously calm. Insecurity overcame the sense of safety I had felt. Solitude gnawed at me like a tumor, a soundless assault. It burned my cold flesh. Death came to the edge of the table and stood there, but I did not know whether I was seeing its back or its face. It was right there. If I stretched out my hand I could touch it; I could feel its presence.

She murmured from a distance: "Send me a letter."

It's not yet too late. I am not ashamed. I could even deny the whole thing, and say that it was an elaborate trick. We can go pike fishing. Heavy bodies, nearly three feet long, must be moving about stealthily under the shade of the water lily leaves in the dark autumn water. I could even go back to Tokyo and sit in my study. This is not Japan's war—the simple, barren thought dawns on me in all its immensity and settles on my heart. The fact that I, who am supposed to be an absolutely free spirit and a liberal, should lean on blood and geographical ties is laughable, but it is true. I want it to be Japan's war. I want it to be the coercion of the state, an absolute command, a mandate. I want my hatred and despair to be given roots. Eulogies that may appear in my obituary flash through my mind and I feel that every one of them has some element of truth; yet their sum total bears no relation to me. All the heroic phrases are too exaggerated and imprecise; they are all too wordy for me to lean on or to use as a springboard. Death is just around the corner, but I am not here. I am between the insect world and the human one, drifting. I have not made up my mind. I have not yet caught up with myself. Without being able to come to any decision, without being able to catch up, thinking that I can retreat at any time, I must depart just as I am, in confusion. The medieval priest lived with a skull on his table to contemplate day and night. I can only imagine the gradual decomposition of my corpse in warm subtropical mud, from the early pale, waxy stages of decay to the final state of gray powder.

"Would you like to go to the park?" she asked.

"I would rather ride an electric train."

"An electric train?"

"The circular line here."

"All right."

She stood up, her face still tender.

Railroad stations are like insect lures with their multicolored flashing lights, but this one was different. As we approached, the boulevard went dark, and shops, lamps, people's shadows, and odors all became indistinguishable. The sound of footsteps only echoed in the empty ditch. In the meager circle of light cast by the streetlamps that stood like lonely toadstools we could see that the concrete of the pavement had cracked here and there and weeds were sprouting through the gaps. The station cast a pall over the entire area; the building itself was also a ruin. The walls were filthy, the doors were cracked, and the odor of stale urine wafted by.

When she went to the window to buy tickets, I finally realized that there was someone inside, but what I saw was a pale blob of mist rather than a face. We climbed the stairs and came out onto the platform. There was no one there, but some circular lights cast a random glow. The light and noise formed a vast tideland under our eyes. She walked away, the sound of her heels an echoing click. Then she crossed the circular halo again, returning out of the darkness. She hunched her neck into her shoulders, as though cold.

"Do you know the poems of Goethe?"

"There are so many."

"You must know this one:

Peace covers the mountain peaks.
You can barely feel a breath of wind stir in the treetops.

This is what that poem was describing."

She opened her clenched fists, gestured vaguely around her and gave a low, mischievous chuckle.

The electric train soon appeared out of the darkness. There were many cars but each box had only one or two passengers in it, and some were completely empty. No one got off, and no one but us got in. We forced the door open and boarded, and the train began to move with a loud squeal. The old iron boxes had aged, but were sturdy and clean. There were no torn newspapers, or candy wrappings scattered about, and no spit on the floor. The linoleum had peeled off here and there and had holes in it, but it was clean. Since no one used the train, nothing got soiled. The cars arrived at one station after another, but all of them were equally empty and desolate. I felt as if there was one single immobile station that the train ran past never-endingly. It was like a ghost ship.

Soon she said: "We are in the East."

And after a while, she said: "We are in the West."

As we remained in our seats, the train continued to circulate endlessly around in the sky above the city. When it crossed into the East, it stopped at the station at the border, but it did not stop anywhere else before it returned to the West. In the West, it stopped at each station and then after a while we were back in the East. There is a technical difference between a local and an express train. But all the stations were equally uninhabited, so the local and the express came to the same thing. The train stopped or continued through obstinately, diligently, accurately, but everything stayed the same. It crossed over and cried "Life!" and passed back and shouted "Death!"

She says: "It's the East."

After a while: "West again."

The East was dark and echoing; and the West was bright and expansive. But as I looked out of the window of the train that stopped, and then ran, stopped, and then ran, without seeing the backs of any passengers getting off or any faces boarding—as I watched, leaning against the hard board of the seat—the darkness gradually brightened, then the glow gradually dimmed. East and West ceased to be distinguishable. I could not tell "Over there" from "Over here." I no longer knew whether the train was running or standing still.

Ten o'clock . . . tomorrow morning . . . the plane to Vietnam.

A Note About the Author

Takeshi Kaiko was born in Osaka, Japan, on December 30, 1930. He is a graduate of Osaka City University's Department of Law. Author of several earlier novels, he has received both Japan's Akutagawa Prize and the Mainichi Culture Prize. *Darkness in Summer* is the first of his novels to be translated into English.

He lives in Tokyo with his wife and daughter.

A Note About the Translator

Cecilia Segawa Seigle was born in Tokyo, Japan. She received her A.B. from Western College for Women and her M.A. from Bryn Mawr College for the study of English, and her Ph.D. from the University of Pennsylvania in the field of Oriental Studies. She is co-translator, with E. Dale Saunders, of Yukio Mishima's *The Temple of Dawn*. In addition to her activity as a translator, Mrs. Seigle is head of the Far Eastern desk of the Franklin Institute Research Laboratories in Philadelphia.